DEDICATION

To the women who did not give up on me, without you I would...

In gratitude to the women who supported me, believing that this workbook was important and that I could write it.

To Etoile, Alice, Harriet, Dorothy, Melanie, Julie, Deborah, Eugenie, and the women of Woodneath Library Writers and KC Writer's groups.

To the women who shared their stories and their courage in emerging into full spiritual citizenship.

To all the women who will be encouraged by this book. May you find the peace, respect and love you deserve.

For my children and grandgirls,
May you never need this book.

Images which do not display credits have not been able to be identified as to source.
To beloved reader, in this book you will find a proven, protected path out of the prison maze of religiously enforced abuse that I and other women have used.

Here is an overview of your path:

Your abuser will use several
METHODS at
different
LEVELS

to create
FEAR, GUILT, AND SHAME
to assure his
POWER AND CONTROL
over you through INTIMIDATION.

He will, if necessary, misuse
FAITH BELIEFS
that he knows you value
as part of this pattern.

TO STOP BEING ABUSED, you will
IDENTIFY his
METHODS at different LEVELS
and learn tools to
RECOGNIZE, REDEFINE, RELABEL, AND RESPOND
to disarm these attacks.

By doing these, you will find ways to
GET FREE AND BEGIN TO RECOVER
as well as
GROW IN YOUR FAITH CONCEPTS AND RELATIONSHIP WITH
GOD.

Whenever you begin to feel you have lost your way while under attack, come back to this page to reorient yourself and move forward.

TABLE OF CONTENTS

INTRODUCTION

My vision for you in this workbook is that you will learn about the tools and process I and other women used to break the bondage of Biblical battering.

This workbook helps you regain your focus on you, what you are experiencing, and helps you rise out of the chaos into the sunlight of safety, freedom and peace.

Are you suffering these stress reactions or changes?

Your health is getting worse (stomach in knots, headaches, unable to eat or eating compulsively, insomnia, uncontrollable crying, inability to think clearly).

You find yourself overreacting to noises (called the startle response).

You walk on eggshells, trying to keep anything from upsetting your partner.

You are more isolated than you used to be, ashamed to let anyone know what is going on. You are afraid for church members to know what is happening.

You have lost friends. You have no money. You are forbidden to work or, if you do work, you have to account to your husband or turn your wages over to him.

You live on an emotional roller coaster. Sometimes he is loving and romantic, then he will get upset and lash out. This pattern is getting more frequent and severe.

You are not free to enjoy the activities you used to.

He constantly says you are wrong. It's <u>always</u> your fault. He uses Bible verses to criticize you.

If you seek support from a church leader, you are told to be a better wife, pray, believe, love, obey or forgive more. You may have been told God is testing you, this is good for your soul, or other words that don't address your need.

You accuse yourself of self-pity, being angry, being too sensitive, not having enough faith, not being a good enough wife.

You constantly doubt yourself or are tormented about what God wants you to do yet unable to see how to make the pain stop.

You are using almost all your energy just managing stress and anxiety.

You spend days and nights on your knees praying to God, to know God's will, to know what to do, how to change, how to help him stop hurting you or your children.

You feel you are at the end of your rope. Something has to change, but you don't know what or how to make it happen.

The turmoil and suffering you are in now is not what you intended when you took your wedding vow. You gave your whole heart to your relationship and then it swirled out of control. You want to follow your faith but you also want this abuse to stop. Like an emotional H-bomb, the first time a woman* experiences verbal or physical abuse from her loved one, her mind feels numb, her stomach turns to liquid, and her heart feels leaden and bleeding. Fear and even terror pour through her body. Her head feels fuzzy; it becomes more difficult to think. She begins to have crying spells or panic attacks. The loving, believing man she thought she knew has disappeared. The orderly world where she knew what to do has turned into chaos. Perhaps worst of all, she may feel disconnected from God. She may feel confused about what God wants her to do.

Her faith doesn't appear to be helping. She is in spiritual torment.

<u>Is this what you are going through?</u>

You once believed in your abilities, your worth, that you were loved. You have lost these as your partner increased his control over you. Like a Chinese finger cuff, the more you work to please him, the tighter you are caught in his system. The emotional roller coaster keeps you locked in the cycle. Walls of anger, fear, isolation and silence surround you.

We went through anxiety, dashed hope, bewilderment, betrayal, frustration, terror, and finally clarity. We overcame fears of abandonment and failure. We tried to please our husbands, work with them, understand them, and help them. We discovered that our understanding of what God wanted for us changed.

We believe in you. God sees you, knows you and loves you. You are worth whatever it takes to be free of abuse wrongly enforced in the name of God. You are not alone.

Other women[2] have been in love with an abusive person who uses the name of God, beliefs and even church leaders to enforce his control. You will read examples of their experiences to see how your experience is not unique and how they got free. He may demand submission in the name of love, faith, being a good wife, God's will, or other labels to keep you under control. It is none of these. It is abuse.

By following the path outlined in the workbook, you will understand what he is doing, regain support and self -worth, grow in your faith, and learn how to escape the prison maze. You can begin in any section of the workbook or go back and forth. Just keep it in a secure place.

There are mentoring programs online, like that at verbalabusejournals.com.

Safety Alert: Computer use can be monitored and is impossible to completely clear. If you are afraid your internet usage might be monitored, call the National Domestic Violence Hotline at 1−800−799−7233 or TTY 1−800−787−3224. Users of web browser Microsoft Edge will be redirected to Google when clicking the "X" or "Escape" button.

You cannot do this alone. You don't need to do this alone. Resources are there, as more understanding about misusing God's name in abuse grows.

*Since 85% of battered victims are women, we are writing from the standpoint of a woman spouse or partner. By changing the pronouns, a man who is being religiously abused can apply the same process for support. However, there is a tendency in some faith systems to put more of a burden on women rather than men for the relationship.

[2] In the 2007 survey of Religious Identification, 76.5% of American adults identify as Christian. Most agree that about 25% of these are women of faith assaulted by their partners. Most stay longer than other battered women because they struggle with faith questions.

^ Margary represents a composite of the true experiences of being Biblically battered that the author and others have reported.

CHAPTER 1: IT'S A PATTERN AND YOU ARE NOT TO BLAME

MARGARY'S

STORY

I always loved Christ. But decades of Bible study and church service did not help me know when I was facing the skills of a manipulator using God's name.

Richard, a Baptist minister, had a knowledge of the Bible, wisdom, and vision that captivated me. Articulate, strong, and insightful, he inspired me. I thought we both wanted to help others. We talked for hours about new Christian service ideas. We would be a team, pooling our abilities, and expand independent churches. He praised my communication skills and my devotion to Christ. Marrying him felt like a safe harbor of loving spiritual work, a holy union. He told me what I wanted to hear. My faith is what this type of person knows how to use.

I didn't ask for what I wanted if it seemed to conflict with what he wanted or what we were doing. Being a "helpmeet", serving my Richard, was God's will. I only looked at what I should do. The more I tried to please him, the worse it got. Finally, every normal desire resulted in increasing abuse.

Any needs I had were accused of obstacles to his ministry. At workshops with other Christian women, he made sure to compare me negatively. I donated my income to our mission work but it wasn't enough. When we had our first child, he demanded hours of marathon Bible studies. He got upset if I had to feed the baby or go to the bathroom. If I reminded him about Bible verses to avoid wrath, he would get even angrier. As my husband/Lord, I was not qualified to correct him. Women were to be silent, "submitting to husbands as unto the Lord." Normal needs were evidence I wasn't a true believer.

After each outburst, there would be romantic reconciliations, but his anger would always build again. Temper tantrums kept me quaking, pleading to know what God wanted me to do. Any of my ideas he didn't want to hear were Satan's work, faithlessness, Jezebel traits, or worse, the "whore of Babylon".

Eventually I wondered if it was possible for one person to be as bad as he said I was. I finally understood his only interest was controlling me, my body and money, and using the name of God to do it.

Are you crying out to God for answers and deliverance but still suffering?

QUESTIONS:

1.   Why is he acting like this? Is this really my fault?
2.   How can I believe…pray…change…love enough to make him stop?
3.   He must be sick. How can I help him heal?
4.   Is it God's will that I stay in this marriage?

Abusers misuse their victim's belief in God to keep them in shame and guilt. This increases their power and control over them. This desire goes beyond what is normal mutual consideration in close relationships. It is deliberate control to hurt you and keep you bound. ***Your faith is being used against you.***

The three main ideas that keep women of faith struggling are
***You believe your thoughts and feelings are somehow wrong or that you don't
        have the right to decide for yourself what is true for you.
The marriage is your responsibility and if it doesn't work you have failed God.
God won't forgive you for breaking a marriage vow.***

By using the steps in this workbook, women have learned that
**   Christ did not die for them to live like this.
        Submitting to an abusive husband is not God's will for them or their
children.
        Jesus wants abundant life for us, which means honoring and using our gifts.**

Damaging Catch-All Concepts

A.   Male privilege (headship)/ Women's Submission

1. <u>To avoid responsibility</u>
    Richard said he was justified in destroying Margary's personal goods as "God's wrath upon the wicked." Whenever she objected to being mistreated, he would blame her for his behavior. She was a constant and convenient scapegoat. He also liked repeating the verse about forgiving 70 x 7 to meet her protests about

his abuse. He rarely if ever forgave and "made her pay" if she didn't do what he wanted. Forgiveness is about not holding resentment, but it doesn't mean continuing to be misused. Rather than change his behavior, Richard used the forgiveness verse to shift responsibility.

2. Underline To sanction self-centeredness

Double standards meant that he sanctioned what we wanted with Bible verses while prohibiting her the same adulthood. Richard's position as a church leader or believer was a catch-all to sanction anything he wanted to do, his desire for money, sex or power.

He insisted on controlling money she earned for his own purposes while she, the children or the house, went without, claiming "the worker is worthy of his hire."

Richard refused to allow friends or family relationships outside the church, misusing the verse about being "contaminated with "the world". His real purpose was to limit the kind of people who would not support his control.

B.   Selective or Incorrect Application of Bible Verses

The idea of "headship" or "leadership" has been both misapplied and incorrectly translated. Claims that women must obey/submit no matter what are not true to the whole word of God. Corresponding verses instructing men to love and cherish their wives are not emphasized. Some will counterclaim that they do not have to honor her because she is not worthy, which means not doing what he wants.

Margary was coerced against her will by constant references to the "Women, obey" verse. She wrote letters to coworkers she did not agree with, signed legal papers she didn't want to, or had sex in painful ways, because of violent threats. Their children witnessed his disrespect and abuse. He would wait until school had already started to enroll them, change schools unnecessarily every year, or embarrass them in the classroom, just to flaunt his authority. Bible study replaced health, friends,

10

or education. Enforced excessive fasting or being spanked for praying "incorrectly" were harmful practices.

He called his right to whip her "Christian discipline". If she did resist him, he yelled she was evil or faithless. Once he used a belt to whip her while she was pregnant with their third child.

C.   Incomplete or Selective View of Redemption

Even if a woman is redeemed, she must continue to suffer, feel guilty, or be punished for her shortcomings. Her sins are worse and the freedom promised her in Christ is limited. She must continue to pay as if she is a second-class soul.

1. No Limit Suffering/Sacrifice

Richard preferred verses that exalted her suffering as praiseworthy. He did not suffer or sacrifice, however. Or he claimed to be sacrificing by tolerating her. This way he turned a teaching into an insult. He liked to teach about fear, trembling, God's wrath. Jesus' love, tolerance, forgiveness, mercy, compassion were overlooked, unless used to criticize her about how she fell short. This created more guilt, shame or intimidation. Objections were met by quoting verses, such as "No greater love has anyone than to lay down his life for his friends" as an expectation for her but not him.

2. Sin is Primarily Women's Fault Because of Her Sexuality

An overemphasis on sex as the major sin means that greater wrongs, like greed, oppression, or war are left unaddressed. Some teach women's bodies are the source of sin. Men's sexual behavior does not come under the same standards. If a man is unfaithful, often the woman is blamed. "Present your bodies as a living sacrifice" and other verses about "the flesh" are more often leveled against a woman. This view contributes to abuse by not holding him responsible if he sexually abuses his wife or children, which is about power and control. When one abused woman, weary of the constant criticism, told her husband that "all have fallen short of the glory of God, he replied, "Yes, but you are the worst of all because you are a woman."

> *You should be aware that all abuse relies upon similar patterns and methods, from verbal abuse to the most extreme physical forms. Abuse begins slowly, subtly and gradually increases. It demoralizes the person until she loses the ability to function without the abuser.*

Margary prayed for over 10 years for God to change her or tell her how to help her abusive husband, a minister. Finally, she stopped groveling and asked God to either change him or release her. When she changed her prayer, her prayer was answered, because God was not pleased with her submitting to this abuse and the damage it was creating. In this way her concept of obedience changed. Was she going to obey her husband or God? The God of her faith made it clear:

1. **Her husband was not living as a believer.**
2. **She is not responsible for his behavior.**
3. **She is not responsible for changing him.**
4. **She is free to refuse any further abuse, so she can live her faith.**

No one who truly loves you would treat you this way. God commands a man love his wife. When he says he is threatening, criticizing or hurting you because he loves you, he is only saying this to keep you controlled. Jesus called people into loving relationships with God and each other. Jesus repeatedly put people's needs before laws and sacrifice.

Abuse is subtle and gradual. The imprisonment involves brainwashing, demoralization, isolation, and other invasions of your soul. Because your faith ideas like dedication are important to you, the abuser will use them to keep you in bondage. Your job will be to mature in your faith to live in the full light and love of God. You will come, like Margary did, to understand that when he uses the Bible, he is not doing it because he wants to live as a Christian.

In this workbook, you will learn and practice tools that Margary used successfully to get free to live her life of faith. The five tools are <u>charting, redefining, journaling, uncovering assumptions, and</u> <u>assertive communication</u>. They bring you through a process that will empower you:

1. **Distancing yourself – stepping back to look at reality, not the abusers distorted view**
2. **Honoring yourself – recovering your lost value, worth and dignity**
3. **Equipping yourself – gaining strength through support and skills**
4. **Freeing yourself – establishing a stronger faith and healthier life**

CHAPTER 2: DEDICATION

When I dedicated myself to Richard, I believed it was what God wanted me to do.

One night I was invited to a friend's house for dinner. About an hour after I got there, the hostess said I had a phone call. It was him, reaming me up one side and down the other for accepting a social invitation without letting him know. I was shaking. I hated conflict and felt called to be a peacemaker so I promised to leave the event. It was the first warning sign, except I had no information that that was what it was. I didn't know it was also my chance to set some boundaries. I was dedicated to pleasing him.

My idea of dedication was wholehearted and my responsibility. I had taken a vow before God. My belief left little room for negotiation or honoring my needs. My heart and mind were at his service. If he stormed out of the house when I wanted to go out with a friend, I believed there must be something missing in my commitment. I would often wait an hour on him, but when I was five minutes late, he would quote Eph 5:16. I should make the best use of time because "the days are evil". I did not tell him the same thing. I accepted it. I was dedicated beyond reason.

Praying on my knees, crying, backing down, pleading, more and more became the pattern of my days and nights. I clung to Bible verses that featured God undertaking against enemies, such as Psalm 91. I had dedicated myself to him and he was standing in the Lord's stead. I didn't want to fail what I promised God I would do.

Are you dedicating yourself to a partner who mistreats you because you want to be faithful to God?

QUESTIONS:

1. *Is this behavior what any husband who is unhappy would do?*
2. *How far should I be punished for making a mistake?*
3. *Is it wrong for me to feel angry when he gets upset with me?*
4. *His words cut me like a knife in my heart. Is this just me being oversensitive?*

Level One- You Don't Know Whether It's Really Abuse

Faith Concept: **Discernment**

In this section you will….

Identify traits of abuse and abusers

Recognize the deliberate use of Fear and Shame for Power and Control

Understand how your dedication is misused

Use charting to record your experience

While some would say that if you ask this question, you are being abused, it is often not that simple for a woman under pressure. Keeping her confused is one of the main abusive methods because it contributes to demoralization. For example, Margary remembers calling a Christian counselor to find out if Richard's slapping her was abuse.

Disconnection from a sense of self was the result of a constant, prolonged onslaught of degrading words and behaviors directed against her.

Abuse occurs along a continuum, from mild to extreme.

    Mild abuse can and often does escalate when not confronted.

Abuse is deliberate and conscious.

    Abuse occurs across social, economic, educational and religious groups.

Abuse occurs in similar patterns no matter whether individual, organizational, or religious body. Abusive tactics share similarities whether used in concentration camps, cults, or other forms of captivity.

It is no less abuse behind the closed doors of a marriage than in a larger setting or organization.

    If anything, isolation without others to share with deepens the damage and difficulty of escape.

Abusers do not take responsibility for the harm they create.

    Abusers use similar tools to keep the victim controlled and accessible. Once the victim escapes and they cannot recapture them, they go on to another victim.

The abuse in the name of God is the most sinister assault on spiritual well- being. It is not the type of spiritual battle that is part of redemptive "testing" by God. Abuse in the name of God is still abuse.

Women in abusive relationships have symptoms of PTSD or CPTSD (Post Traumatic Stress Disorder or Complex Post Traumatic Stress Disorder) like combat veterans. These symptoms are real and should not be ignored. If you are told to "just pray, believing" "give it to God" "ignore it and it will go away" "buck up" or other words that don't take your wellbeing seriously, realize that the person advising this is not the one suffering. CPTSD is discussed in Chapter 9.

Abusive Traits

Does your partner show…
- A sense of entitlement, grandiosity, rules don't apply to him
- A charismatic personality, subtly manipulative
- Controlling, self-absorbed (a narcissistic person)
- Projects motives on others
- Refuses to take responsibility for his part in relationship
- Either-or; all-or-nothing thinking, absolutes dominate
- Isolation, total devotion required for relationship, no privacy allowed
- Motivated by a desire for power, sex, money cloaked in religious terms

Recognize the Deliberate Use of Fear and Shame for Power and Control

The abuser manipulates your dedication to love and service for his benefit, a "wolf in sheep's clothing" pattern of relating. You believe what he says. The abuser uses this belief against you.

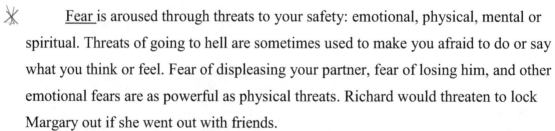

Fear is aroused through threats to your safety: emotional, physical, mental or spiritual. Threats of going to hell are sometimes used to make you afraid to do or say what you think or feel. Fear of displeasing your partner, fear of losing him, and other emotional fears are as powerful as physical threats. Richard would threaten to lock Margary out if she went out with friends.

Shame is aroused by words and teachings that reject who you are as a person. The message is that you are not just someone with a problem or who made a mistake.

Shame is a pervasive feeling that you <u>are</u> a mistake, that your existence is the problem. There is no recourse for shame. Margary's husband often called her "Devil's Daughter" or "Spawn of the Devil" if she didn't do what he wanted. These labels are an insult against her as a person, not just as someone with faults. It was meant to make her feel totally condemned as a person.

<u>Guilt</u> is aroused by words and teachings that emphasize judgement and often result   ✳ from shame messages. The abuser may accuse you of doing something wrong but will not allow you to correct the mistake or will not accept your apology. This sets up an agonizing reaction in a person of conscience like yourself. You turn yourself inside out or wrack your brain trying to figure out how to make it up to him.

Richard would tell Margary he wouldn't be home for supper and then would come home and ask why supper wasn't ready. If she would try to apologize or fix him supper, he would sulk, not talk, or leave to eat elsewhere. He wanted to make her feel guilty. Her dedication would then get stronger. She would try harder to anticipate what he might want the next time. This kept her feeling anxious and drained physically, emotionally, mentally and spiritually. He would then shame her by calling her worthless.

<u>When you get into this spiral of fear, shame and guilt, he has power and control over you.</u>

Let's examine how he consciously uses fear and shame for power and control in your relationship. The **major methods** fall into four categories for you to recognize. I and others have experienced all of them. A Bible verse can be used to reinforce these methods.

A. <u>Demoralizing and Accusing Words</u>
- He calls you degrading names. These may be vulgur, sexually contemptuous, or names of Biblical women like Jezebel.
- Accuses you of lying or falsely accuses you in other ways.
- Dismisses or mocks your ideas and feelings.
- Insults your intelligence, talents, skills, or beliefs.
- Flirts, compares you negatively to other women; criticizes your body or compares it to theirs.
- Sabotages birth control; threatens to leave; insists he has the right to have sex with others.

B. Denying or Minimizing His Behavior; One Way Relationship
- Says you would do things you do not want to if you loved him.
- Sulks. Explodes. Silent treatment. Withholds affection.
- Refuses responsibility for his part in relationship.
- Says you are too sensitive, he was just kidding, etc.
- Says he is Christ's presence on earth and cannot be reproached. Your "lord" and not to be questioned.
- Has a Bible verse ready to chide you with if you counter his views.
- Insists you must submit but he is free to do as he pleases (called a double standard)

C. Playing the Victim, Refusing to Take Responsibility
- Says you don't care about him if you expect adult behavior.
- Reminds you of how mistreated he has been or other excuses not to be held accountable.
- Nothing is his fault; it's your or someone else's fault.
- Pattern of past failed relationships.
- Says God delivers him, only God can judge, or uses other rationalizations rather than make amends for wrongs.
- Counters with a Bible verse to correct you if you express a need.
- Claims he's just trying so hard and no one understands him.
- Withholds affection or demands sex as a way to enforce control.
- Says you're the only one who can help him.
- Claims to be so hurt and upset because he cares so much that he just loses control (e.g. you made him do it).
- Cites women like Abigail who calmed man's wrath.

D. Threatening Behaviors
- Leaves you locked out or refuses to let you leave.
- Takes your money or uses your accounts without your permission. Strictly watches "allowance" or does not allow you to have money.
- Monitors your movements or phone calls.
- Blocks doorways or corners or pins you against the wall. Pins you down.
- Destroys items of value to you. Punches wall or destroys objects. Throws objects.
- Uses bodily gestures to instill fear: raises a hand to make you flinch; points or shakes finger close in your face.
- Grabs your arm, hand or other body part with a force that bruises.
- Disturbs your sleep; keeps you up for long hours; accuses you of being lazy if you need sleep.

18

Many abusers today are now aware of penalties for physical abuse. Even if they limit bruises and other harm to parts of the body that are hidden, it is too risky that these can be detected. Therefore more abusers are majoring in psychological (mental, emotional, and verbal) and spiritual intimidation through fear, shame and guilt to enforce bondage e.g. power and control. This has resulted in many operating in church settings where women dedicated to serving others are found.

Identify How Your Faith Is Just Another Tool for an Abuser

Your dedication can be misused by this type of personality in several ways. That is because women of faith are trying to live a good life pleasing to God. We are idealistic and usually want to work for a better world. We tend to be giving and compassionate. We want to give people the benefit of the doubt or second chances. We want to uplift others.

An abuser finds this type of person an ideal target. Our dedication results in our reluctance to challenge what is happening to us. We tend to try to be even more dedicated, thinking we are failing if he is acting this way.

Abusers actually are attracted to talented, strong, and intelligent women. They find the challenge of conquering them appealing. A common way they do this is to humiliate, confuse, or sadden them and then accuse them of having emotional or mental issues that cause the distress. The goal is to get you to blame yourself. In faith groups, they like to urge you to "confess your sins one to another." There are no social or economic classes, professions or belief groups where such individuals are not found, although some systems are easier for them to operate in than others.

An abusive manipulator is skilled at misusing verses and faith concepts to make you feel guilty, challenge you, dismiss you, or demoralize you because of your desire to please God. If you are targeted for control, you will find that your dedication to do good, be caring, or live your ideals is used against you. Because these ideals are hard to pin down, words like "faith," "forgiveness," "doing the will of God," "sacrifice," and being "Christ-like" are used like bludgeons to keep you under control. Guilt and shame for your reasonable and normal desires and behaviors become the weapon of choice. A Biblically battered woman is suffering under this misuse which denies normal human consideration, not to mention the love and dignity Christ showed women.

One woman explained that predators assume churches will protect their reputation over that of victims, are reluctant to involve police or outside professionals, use unequal power structures, and major in abstractions or non-verifiable concepts. These conditions work in an abuser's favor. (@ashleymeaster, #churchtoo, Twitter, November 23, 2017).

Joy-- not suffering-- is the portal to the divine.

Julia Cameron

They know the woman or girl will be blamed in most cases and asked to repent for their part in the violation.

If you find that scriptures or teachings are being used to create pain in your life, your fellow Christians, both men and women, may not understand. They might continue to tell you to pray, be a better wife, believe, and submit, or accept his "repentence" repeatedly. You may be one of countless women whose current church was not the refuge they needed. While more leaders understand the abuse syndrome today, others may still rather uphold obedience than confront the sin of abuse. Some leaders deny the problem because they are uncomfortable with it or do not know how to help. Unfortunately, church members can be committed to upholding male privilege at the expense of the woman's welfare.

The Primary Weapon: VERBAL ABUSE
adapted from Patricia Evans, <u>The Verbally Abusive Relationship</u>

Verbal abuse is the most spiritually destructive, cutting your very spirit. Many women report that verbal abuse is worse than physical because it goes to the soul, eroding and killing your spirit, and can be more painful than a stabbing. Verbal abuse is emotional soul cutting, aging you quickly and robbing you of your inner defenses.

It is the foundation and most used weapon in the abuser's arsenal.

These methods are especially difficult to deal with because the skilled abuser phrases them in a way that makes them difficult to counter.
Examples are:

Withholding *– a purposeful, silent treatment*
Countering- *pretending to misunderstand what you have said and attempting to refute your ideas, feelings or perceptions*

Discounting- *putting down what you say or hold dear*
Blocking and diverting- *covert way of violating your dignity*

Accusation and blame- *lying about your intentions, attitudes and motives*
Judging and criticizing *–lying about your personal qualities and performance*

Trivializing and undermining- *making light of your work, effort, interests or concerns; diluting the meaning or value of your life; undermining can involve joking at your expense or when you are hurt; sometimes used with discounting, to avoid admitting the joke was meant to be mean*

Name calling- *verbal abuse by definition*
Ordering- *telling, not asking, you to do something or making one- way decisions that affect you both without your input*

Deliberate forgetting or denial- *avoiding responsibility by pretending not to remember*
Abusive anger- *using rage, yelling, or other displays to dominate, control, put down, or establish one-upmanship; reactions beyond the seriousness of the issue*

Threatening- *in order to manipulate, threatening to leave, stay out all night, take you home immediately, etc. This creates an emotional dread or terror of impending chaos or disaster that is meant to shatter the partner's serenity and boundaries.*

It's a Cycle...

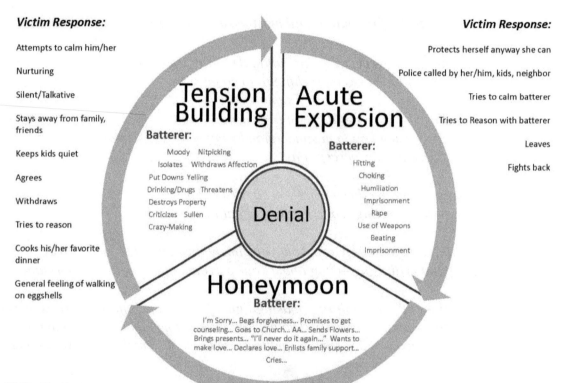

Victim Response:

Attempts to calm him/her

Nurturing

Silent/Talkative

Stays away from family, friends

Keeps kids quiet

Agrees

Withdraws

Tries to reason

Cooks his/her favorite dinner

General feeling of walking on eggshells

Victim Response:

Protects herself anyway she can

Police called by her/him, kids, neighbor

Tries to calm batterer

Tries to Reason with batterer

Leaves

Fights back

Tension Building

Batterer:

Moody   Nitpicking
Isolates   Withdraws Affection
Put Downs Yelling
Drinking/Drugs Threatens
Destroys Property
Criticizes   Sullen
Crazy-Making

Acute Explosion

Batterer:

Hitting
Choking
Humiliation
Imprisonment
Rape
Use of Weapons
Beating
Imprisonment

Denial

Honeymoon

Batterer:

I'm Sorry... Begs forgiveness... Promises to get counseling... Goes to Church... AA... Sends Flowers... Brings presents... "I'll never do it again..." Wants to make love... Declares love... Enlists family support... Cries...

Victim Response:

Agrees to stay, returns, or takes batterer back.... Attempts to stop legal proceedings... Sets up for counseling appointments for batterer... Feels Happy, Hopeful

Center for Family
Violence Prevention

POWER AND CONTROL

PHYSICAL   VIOLENCE   SEXUAL

USING COERCION AND THREATS
Making and/or carrying out threats to do something to hurt her • threatening to leave her, to commit suicide, to report her to welfare • making her drop charges • making her do illegal things.

USING INTIMIDATION
Making her afraid by using looks, actions, gestures • smashing things • destroying her property • abusing pets • displaying weapons.

USING EMOTIONAL ABUSE
Putting her down • making her feel bad about herself • calling her names • making her think she's crazy • playing mind games • humiliating her • making her feel guilty.

USING ECONOMIC ABUSE
Preventing her from getting or keeping a job • making her ask for money • giving her an allowance • taking her money • not letting her know about or have access to family income.

USING MALE PRIVILEGE
Treating her like a servant • making all the big decisions • acting like the "master of the castle" • being the one to define men's and women's roles

USING ISOLATION
Controlling what she does, who she sees and talks to, what she reads, where she goes • limiting her outside involvement • using jealousy to justify actions.

USING CHILDREN
Making her feel guilty about the children • using the children to relay messages • using visitation to harass her • threatening to take the children away.

MINIMIZING, DENYING AND BLAMING
Making light of the abuse and not taking her concerns about it seriously • saying the abuse didn't happen • shifting responsibility for abusive behavior • saying she caused it.

PHYSICAL   VIOLENCE   SEXUAL

DOMESTIC ABUSE INTERVENTION PROJECT

202 East Superior Street
Duluth, Minnesota 55802
218-722-2781
www.duluth-model.org

 *Tool One: Cut Through the Maze with Charting*

Charting is a way to begin to distance yourself from the chaos or emotional suffering you are experiencing.

Battering is a cyclic behavior following a predictable path. Some women have even found it follows monthly patterns.

You begin by keeping a record for a week or a month of the episodes in the cycle of abuse: the honeymoon, the rising tension, the triggering incident and explosion, and the lull afterward.

Record what is said, your response, and his reaction. What does he gain from the behavior? What does he do? Do his actions match what he says?

You will begin to see a pattern emerge. You will recognize methods that your partner uses repeatedly. By seeing the pattern, you can begin to recognize how it is consistently used to create fear, guilt and shame in you for being yourself and increase his power and control to get his way.

With your chart or calendar, begin keeping a list of your faith beliefs that your partner uses against you to justify his mistreatment of you. You may be aware of many of these beliefs, but you will be able to put things together you did not realize before by keeping a chart. You will see that what he does actively works against your wellbeing: physical, emotional, mental, or spiritual. Many women are surprised at the frequency or severity of what the chart reveals. They were not aware of how very much they are being subjected to. Then identify which category they are examples of. You will practice charting in the Exercise that follows.

CHAPTER TWO: EXERCISE

Here you will begin listing the disturbing words and behaviors that are going on, using the four categories of methods in this chapter. Label what happens as an example of

A. Demoralizing and Accusing Words

B. Denying or Minimizing His Behavior; One Way Relationship

C. Playing the Victim, Refusing to Take Responsibility

or D. Threatening Behaviors

What is his payoff for what he does?

<u>Power</u> – he is able reinforce his place, his desires, right to be the final word, make the final decision, even if it disregards your wellbeing.

<u>Control</u> – he is able to prevent or make you do something damaging he wants against your will

<u>Intimidation</u> – he is able to weaken your inner self, confidence, or any of your adult abilities: mental, physical, emotional or spiritual ability

Example:

Monday: Describe what happened._____

He called me a lazy slut when I didn't vacuum the floor. An example of **A: Demoralizaing and Accusing Words**

Check how you were affected: __x_Mental __x_Emotional
_____Physical____x__Spiritual
What you felt: ____fear ___x_ guilt ___x_ shame ____anger ___ other: shocked
What he gained: _____power ____x_ control ___x__intimidation

Here is a space to begin your examples. Be sure to identify any of the **4 categories** that your experience is part of. **(A, B, C, and/or D above)**

Monday: Describe what happened._____

An example of _____

Check how you were affected: ___Mental _____Emotional_____Physical_____Spiritual

What you felt: ____fear ____ guilt ____ shame ____anger ___ other

What he gained: _____power _____ control

Tuesday:

_____

An example of _____

This damaged my _____mental_____emotional_____physical_____spiritual wellbeing

What you felt: ____fear _____guilt_____shame____ anger_____other_____

What he gained: ____ power over _____control over_____

Continue this way for the week or up to a month.

Then tally what number of time you were diminished in each way:

____**A: Demoralizing and Accusing Words**

____**B: Denying or Minimizing His Behavior; One Way Relationship**

____**C: Playing the Victim, Refusing to Take Responsibility**

____**D: Threatening Behaviors**

please take one!

because you're adorable | for your sweet personality | to match your beautiful smile

you deserve to feel loved.

TINY DEVOTIONS

Now take some time to review what you have learned. Summarize it here:

My Prayer: "Dear God, I know you love me. You know I want to be a good wife. You know how hurt I am. I want to do Your will. Help me stop being dishonest about what is really going on. Help me be able to step back and see more clearly. I want peace. I need comfort. I believe in your goodness. My soul cries out to you, 'Help me believe my inheritance of your kingdom lives within'. Amen."

"The very qualities Christian women are encouraged to cultivate are the very qualities that are most attractive to abusive men." -Barbara Roberts, "Waking the Evangelical Church to Domestic Violence and Abuse in Its Midst".

https://cryingoutforjustice.com

CHAPTER 3: DEVOTION

My dedication grew into blind devotion. Perhaps I deserved this treatment as a test of my devotion.

I began to ask myself whether somehow I deserved it. He knew how to convince me I did. I ended up a hostage in our car at times, with him screaming at me about my incompetency, worthlessness, and sinfulness and leaving me in crying confusion.

He twisted many Bible verses to intimidate me. I believed all our problems were my fault. Accusations of being faithless, selfish, even evil were constant. Each time he used these, I would question what God wanted me to do.

God was such an easy term for him to throw around, stopping my mind and targeting my heart's desire to be a good wife. The nagging question was always: Am I failing as a wife, as a Christian?

When I wanted to use some of the money I earned for my own needs, I was upbraided as not willing to support God's work. When I wanted to sleep instead of have sex, I was shirking my marriage duty. No matter what, if it conflicted with what he wanted, he said I was displeasing God. If I was displeasing God, then I deserved this treatment. So the cycle reinforced itself. His tirades grew longer, reinforcing that there was something wrong with me and wearing me down mentally, emotionally and physically.

The emotional damage was still operating underneath. A religious abuser knows how to capture a believing victim. I had married the accuser who, as Revelations explained, accuses believers night and day before God. (Rev. 12:210)

Rather than accept constant upbraiding, my challenge began to be clarifying my faith and understanding his verbal manipulation. When I did, I realized I was not doing anything so wrong that I deserved this abuse.

Are you trapped in the lie that somehow you deserve his abuse?

QUESTIONS

1. *Are the things he says about me true?*
2. *What have I done to make him behave like this?*
3. *How can I change to stop him from being upset?*
4. *Is this how I am to "work out my salvation in fear and trembling?"*
5. *Is God not answering my prayers because I have failed?*

In the last section, you learned how to identify abuse. You now understand you are being abused. This takes away some of your confusion. Each abused woman thinks she is the only one living like this. But it is a widespread problem.

In this chapter you will...
   Recognize that feeling you deserve abuse is part of the abuse
    Redefine the meaning of the submission.
   Relabel the messages to begin to regain self-worth

The path is a gradual one. Margary questioned whether she deserved it because she feared falling short. She believed Richard when he said, for example, she couldn't manage on her own or that it's his way or no way. Under the mental attacks, she lost focus on the Christ of her experience, who loved her unconditionally and equally, forgave imperfections, and promised her "my yoke is easy and my burden is light."

You may begin to betray yourself to survive. When he won't stop accusing you of lying, for example, you may finally lie, saying that you lied, to stop the harassment. It is a very complicated game. But betraying yourself adds to your idea that you deserve the abuse.

Your chart gives you a way to see this manipulation and stop blaming yourself. Instead of focusing on each separate crisis, you find out your partner knows what he is doing. Even throwing a tantrum is used just for the effect on you. It is *hard to* believe, but we discovered that our abusive partners turn their anger on and off when it suited them. They enjoyed keeping us on an emotionally roller coaster. It fit in with using guilt, fear and shame for power and control.

Now we want to extend what we began in the previous section. Since you clearly know it is abuse, you now want to want to get free of the idea that you deserve the abuse.

We will find out why this happened and how to escape it to live again in God's love.

LEVEL 2 - You Know It's Abuse But You Wonder If You Deserve It

Faith Concept: Submission (Evidenced by Obedience)

Why would you think you deserved such treatment? Here are what others have explained about how hard it is to sort out.

<u>We didn't know what was a reasonable effort.</u>

The ideal of giving until it hurt, sacrificially or until death was an engrained expectation. "Nothing but the best for God" was our mantra even in childhood. An impossible standard of love as "bearing all things" became a source of guilt when we couldn't measure up.

A spiritual perfectionism locked us in. Even if we didn't' do anything wrong, our determination to "help" or fix the situation would kick in. If we couldn't fix it, that was evidence we had failed. We were mired in struggle and turmoil.

<u>We believed that the relationship was mainly our responsibility.</u>

Our purpose was to help others live their best lives. We didn't question one-way relationships where we did all the giving. We always questioned ourselves first. Too often we thought being peacemakers meant not asking for anything ourselves if it inconvenienced someone else. Finally, our pride prevented us from admitting we couldn't make it work.

<u>We feared rejection or abandonment if we didn't do what others wanted.</u>

Verses like "no man putting his hand to the plow" became sources of dread. "Either/or" or "all or nothing" thinking closed many reasonable options. If a woman begins to question or resist the abuse, her abuser may switch tactics. This keeps her off balance. He will try being Mr. Right, Mr. Victim, or Mr. Suave. If upbraiding her doesn't work, he may whine or cry that she is mistreating him or doesn't care about him. Or he may try romance. If that doesn't work, he may threaten to leave or leave for a short time until she submits to his manipulation. Some threaten suicide.

But mainly we couldn't get past the constant command to submit. But submitting never solves the problem. So we felt like a failure, and if we failed, we believed we must be punished. But this is not the Christ of our faith.

Submission is a responsibility that is placed solely on women in the relationship. The idea of male privilege, which Jesus did not teach, is the excuse. If she doesn't cower, he says, it's a sin. If she is sinning by not submitting, he is allowed to punish her.

This twisted thinking makes injustice godly. It seeks to remove the salvation through Christ that we have as believers.

Jesus scandalized religious leaders by extending respect for women in his behavior. The belief in male privilege does not uphold this teaching. Those who insist on her submission do not hold the abuser responsible. Instead they expect her to fix the problem, "bear patiently" with it, or offer it up to the glory of God. They dismiss her with a pat on the head and an exhortation to "pray and believe." The abuser is not held responsible; his victim is blamed.

Abusers have no trouble assuming God's role in her life. They disrespect her boundaries, personal freedom and dignity. Uninformed Christians may tell the abuser to repent but they do not free the woman. Too often they do not understand what their insistence on saying together means. It extends access to the victim and prolongs the abuse.

"Obedience" is a favorite tool abusers use to bully the women in a relationship, an easy weapon for a tyrant to wield to get his way without having to justify it, a tool for any demand, no matter how unreasonable. This is not the concept of obedience that Jesus taught. Obedience does not require losing your health, your sanity, your peace, your overall ability to care for your children if you have them.

Is there a valid reason that this teaching should be emphasized more than other teachings that men should love their wives as Christ loved the church?

Whatever you believe, the abuser thinks obedience is a handy club to keep you submissive. While you are wondering if you deserve being mistreated, asking God and pleading for answers, the abuser keeps using your desire to please God against you. We have to make sense of all of the Bible, not just a few verses given more importance to uphold someone's power over another. An abuser is no longer acting as God commands in the relationship. He has broken the vow to love. The contract is null and void. You did not vow to obey an abuser when you married.

 *Tool Two: Cut Through the Maze with Labeling*

Abusers deliberately create chaos, bewilderment and confusion. This helps them avoid responsibility for their behaviors by constantly blaming someone else. Their partners begin to feel they deserve the mistreatment.

Abusers have mastered gaslighting by using **no-wins, deflection and projection** to blame their victims and tell them they deserve the mistreatment. A **no-win demand or double-bind statement** is one in which, no matter what you choose, you will lose. Sometimes these are known as Catch 22s. Biblical battering itself is based on a primary no-win: by forbidding a woman to not submit in an abusive marriage and condemning her if she resists, she loses both ways. If she submits, she gets mistreated by her husband. If she resists, she may get mistreated by her church.

Double-standards are related to double-binds. A double-standard means that privilege, ability or power is allowed one person and not the other who is an equal partner. For example, your partner expects to be able to not come home at night but calls you or tracks you from your work to your home and forbids you to go out with friends.

Deflecting means avoiding admitting his behavior by accusing you of not being obedient or some other label not related to his behavior. You may ask him why he is late and he begins to harangue you about the floor needing to be swept. Some men habitually raise their voice and act upset to intimidate their partners so they don't have to ever explain. His reaction goes beyond what is reasonable for the situation.

Projecting means that he will accuse or blame you for what is true of him. Richard routinely accused Margary of being unfaithful, which created enormous pain for her. She found out years later he was cheating at those times when he would accuse her.

These are common and regular in the daily life of the abusive relationship.

No-wins, **deflections** or **projections** accuse you of not being submissive or obedient. He knows this idea important to your faith system. These are effective methods to create your sense of worthlessness because you can't do anything right to please him.

What patterns do you see in your relationship? Are there standards that are hurtful or demoralizing?

Richard would tell Margary to leave the light on for him if he was coming home late but if she did he complained about the electric bill, stormed around the house for a half an hour, and withheld money from the housing allowance, all reactions meant to punish her, not save on the electric bill. If a person is regularly "locked into" a no-win about a variety of issues with a person they care about, it will wear them down, which is the purpose.

Another time he screamed at her for buying a pair of shoes he did not authorize. At that time Margary was donating most of her salary to his "missionary" work. She finally had to face that he wanted to be free to spend money without accounting to her. "God gave you the ability to earn that money," he said. "You owe it to give it back to God." (meaning his ministry). There was one standard for his use of our money and another for Margary, that is, she was not to have any of her earnings.

Now that you have learned how to chart, take some time to look objectively at what happens when you obey or when he says you deserve the abuse. Often what happens is that, even if you obey, it will not change his abusive behavior to you. That tells you that his main goal is creating fear, guilt and shame to maintain his power and control. It also tells you that you do not deserve the abuse, because you are doing your best to be a loving supportive wife.

Danni Moss reports she found the book *Boundaries: When to Say Yes, How to Say No to take Control of Your Life*, by Henry Cloud and John Townsend eye-opening. It enabled her to step back and disengage from her husband's verbal abuse, which then enabled her to respond to it according to what would be reasonable in a relationship.

She also reported "I disagree with 'Lord, change me' first attitude and humble spirit. That is what keeps people in the marriage. I Tim. 5:8 says a man who does not provide for his family (provision = financial, spiritual, emotional protection and leadership) **has denied the faith** and is **worse** than an unbeliever. God calls an unrepentant abusive spouse an unbeliever. 'The anger of man does not accomplish the righteousness of God.' – James 1:20.

Not understanding the nature of non -physical abuse contributes to the inability to cope or confront it. Abused Christian women believe that if they can get him to see what he was doing he will stop. Such is not reality."

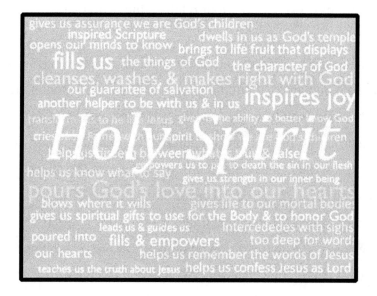

CC B N N unknown

CHAPTER THREE: EXERCISES

Now let's practice redefining and relabeling the accusations and charges made by looking at what is reasonable. This will free you from believing you somehow deserve abuse.

Identify the Tactic, Redefine and Relabel

Redefining and Relabeling

<u>List the words or phrases he uses</u>. For each one, identify the tactic. These contain broad labels and do not have facts. Example: burning toast does not make you a lousy wife. **Is this accusation a _____no win/double bind _____deflection _____ projection**?

You can tell by your lurching gut feeling when these are not true of you. They feel foreign and are not how you behave. An objective observer would confirm this. Challenge each one in your mind by redefining or redirecting them.

Example: "You never listen to me. I try and try but you keep on being a faithless, unbelieving and disobedient wife."

Redefine, redirect in your mind: "Is it true that I never listen to him? I agree with him, ask him questions, try to comfort him. In fact, it is only when I don't agree with him that he says I don't listen to him and accuses me with these labels.

"It is not disobedient to be who I am. He said when he married me, he loved me just the way I am. It is not possible for anyone in a relationship to be the only one responsible for the trouble as he says I am. Obedience does not keep him from mistreating me. He is increasingly demanding I obey him as a god rather than God.

"What he seems really to be saying is that obeying him means always having things his way, and even if I try that, he still hurts me. This is not the mutual support of a healthy relationship. It is not what God gave as a guide for us."

Relabel: "When he accuses me of being disobedient, I realize it is because he wants his way all the time. When he accuses me of being faithless, it is because he means I shouldn't question any of his desires. He accuses me of being unbelieving, because I am not 'believing' only his version of things. If he can continue to use my belief in God to make me feel bad or like a failure, it isn't good for me."

Look back at the information about abuse and your previous charting work.
How often does he use **no-wins/double binds**? _____regularly _____once in a while _____ rarely

How often does he **deflect**? _____regularly _____once in a while _____ rarely

How often does he **project**? _____regularly_____once in a while _____rarely

Do you see evidence of gaslighting, "crazymaking"? (p 43)

Which verbal abuse methods are being used?

| **Withholding____Countering___ Discounting_____Blocking and diverting_____** |
| **Accusation and blame-_____Judging and criticizing _____** |
| **Trivializing and undermining- _____Name calling____Ordering- _____** |
| **Deliberate forgetting or denial- ____Abusive anger- _____Threatening- _____** |

Is this behavior part of fear _____guilt ____, shame,____ enforcing power____ or control _____?

Is this behavior part of a belief in male privilege_____, women are morally inferior and cannot trust their own judgement_____, suffering is a Christian virtue, especially for women, ____forgiveness and reconciliation are a woman's duty._____

Which classic abusive behaviors are happening?
Isolation____Intimidation_____Threats_____Using Children___Sexual Abuse___Economic Abuse___Emotional Abuse___Physical Abuse____Spiritual Abuse_____

What parts of your faith experience or relationship with God are being threatened ?

Now, take up to five more accusations around not submitting or being obedient and work the redefining and relabeling process on each one.

Obedience to God results in living in peace, love, and the rest of the fruits of the Spirit. God does not command obedience to a tyrant, to dishonoring yourself, or to any other ways that misuse Jesus' words to create pain.

Categories and Phrases

Here are categories of statements that are meant to be hard to answer and phrases I and others have found helpful to use with them.

Attribution – a label with no specifics Ex.:You are so lazy.	Refuse to be silent, stonefaced, or uncommitted
Mystification -saying something is real when it isn't Ex: You never cook	Confront with the reality of the situation repeatedly
Entrapment – assuming guilt Ex: When did you stop loving me?	Make expectations explicit.
Punishment – assuming the right to coerce someone to correct them Ex: You will be sleeping on the couch for contradicting me.	The "punishment" must be consistent with the importance of the "offense". (This is not warranted between adults Can verge on sadism).
Overload – keeping a person worn down with excessive demands. Ex: Take the kids to Bible study, then cook dinner, then meet my parents afterward, and then help me with my term paper for Bible History.	Communicate what is enough and insist on privacy to recharge.

Pressuring you for a quick "yes" or "no" answer is another troubling tactic. Here are helpful phrases that can give room to think, breathe, or regain control. Whether or not they are regarded, they still create some space for you to regroup.

"Let me think about that."
"I'll get back to you in a half hour."
"Ok, but I need some time to myself right now."
"No, I haven't found that that works for me very well."
"My policy is…"
"Thanks, but…"
"I can appreciate what you are saying, but…"
"I'll call you back."

Letter to Abuser:

_____

_____

My Prayer: "Dear God, I walk with you in this path. I am doing the best I can. Help me understand more clearly what your vision for my fullness of life is. I know you have created the world in love and abundance. I know you command lovingkindness. I am beginning to see how your message was misused to subject me to men against your will. There is no more sacrifice to be made. Help me learn to live in the freedom of your love. Amen"

"No system, no matter how godly its goal sounds, that carries with it oppression, silencing, de-humanizing, violence, abuse and corruption is healthy." Dr. Diane Langberg

A Brief Look at Communication Games

Being able to step back, analyze our conversations, and see the patterns helped me to understand what my husband was doing that kept me feeling hopeless, a failure, and in despair. If I could not communicate with him, how were we going to work it out? I learned, for all his emphasis on communicating, he wasn't interested. It was just a game.

Communication games are a way to manage others without relating honestly. They are different from authentic communication in a healthy relationship because the goal is not really to solve the problem. In fact, players can get upset if the problem is solved. They are left feeling empty, even depressed because they don't know how to relate any other way.

Each game is based on people assuming a role. People can change roles. My husband would be a persecutor or a rescuer, but both these roles required a victim. If these didn't work, he would pretend to be the victim, accuse me of mistreatment him. Or he would want me to rescue him from his irresponsible behavior. I would lose out, no matter which way he used.

Here are the most prevalent games my husband used, with or without Bible verses. There are many more games that you can find by researching "unhealthy communication games".

"Why Don't You…Yes But"
This game involves pretending to want help but every thing that the person suggests is meant with some reason why it won't work. The point of this communication game is to stay stuck, either helpless, or to keep the other person from having any influence. The person gets to be the center of attention and feels vindicated that no one can help them.

If your abuser does this, refuse to rescue by asking him what he thinks would work and not continuing to give pointless advice.

"Blemish"
Fault-finding keeps everyone focused on someone else's behavior, looking in another direction, so the attention is not on the person doing harm. This person behaves arrogantly so he won't have to face his fears.

If your abuser does this, confront with the pattern and assure them that it is normal to have things that challenge us personally. "Yesterday you criticized me 5 times about…." "Last week, I tried three days to fix you a dinner you would like and nothing worked." Most of the time an abuser will deny this but you have the data from your charts.

"Uproar"
One of my husband's favorites. If he could throw a fit, raise his voice, threaten me, he didn't have to answer or do anything else so issues never got resolved.

Do not engage the person. Walk away. Explain you will come back or talk when the person has calmed down. Do not apologize or take responsibility for his feelings because you will notice he can turn his upset off and on easily based on what he is trying to do.

CHAPTER 4: DELUSION

MARGARY'S STORY

To question my devotion would be falling short and painful. I wrestled with what to do. I didn't understand that a marriage vow didn't cover all of God's will.

Richard was happy to convince me that accepting what he was doing was God's will. I didn't get medical care when I had a serious allergic reaction on a mission trip because it would be a lack of faith. I didn't get prenatal care with my son because the money needed to be used for "the work". If he accused me of being unfaithful, which broke my heart, I thought I should increase my proof of my devotion. After all, didn't God say I should forgive any hurt or betrayal? Wasn't I supposed to sacrifice? Wasn't I supposed to be willing to suffer without complaining to follow Christ? Didn't Christians put their egos aside to help others?

I stood by while my children suffered because I thought God's will was obedience. He struck our five-year-old son for not reading or our three-year-old daughter for not praying in the correct way. When our son left his bike on the front step to come in for dinner and it was stolen, he whipped him, blaming him, not the thief.

I took whatever ridiculous command or reprimand he used and assumed I must handle it, tucking it away under broad ideals about being a Christian. I overlooked the second part of the Great Commandment, loving your neighbor "as yourself".

Self-reliance without self-love left me open to mistreatment. None of this was God's will for me. I had made a vow and didn't realize it was broken. He said he was Christian, but it was because he knew I wanted to follow God and it gave him control.

Do you think God's will does not include your or your children's safety and wellbeing? Does your God desire life or death?

QUESTIONS:

1.   Is my suffering in this marriage part of God's plan for me?

2.   Is my husband working to help me perfect my soul?   A trial by fire?

3.   Is obeying someone who is hurting me helping me spiritually?

4.   My church leader says I need to bear with all things in faith.   Does this apply to my husband' abuse too?

LEVEL 3 – You Know You Don't Deserve It but You Wonder If It Is Somehow God's Will

Faith Concept: God's Will

In this chapter you will…

Recognize the three goals behind your partner's methods
Define how attempts to cope have damaged your life as a woman of faith.
Begin to use journaling to clarify and grow your understanding of God's Will

In the last section, you learned why you do not deserve abuse. The motive for abuse has nothing to do with God. Still a woman of faith has a desire to do God's will. The idea of **forbearance** is important to her. She is willing to forbear at times if she believes it will benefit others. In this way, every idea that she believes is involved to live the life of a believer can become a source of guilt if it is out of balance.

Her next challenge is to determine whether somehow her abuse might somehow be part of God's will for her or her family. Forbearance is one of the ideals but others are the idea of being tested in your faith, verses like "working out your salvation with fear and trembling," and bearing our cross. Emphasis on this verse takes away from the power of Christ's work. It is based on performance rather than faith. It emphasizes your earning your salvation. So you are put on a faith treadmill, always trying to reach a goal that Christ has already given you. Jesus challenged legalism used to oppress others. It made him angry.

Your abuser is not concerned with doing any of these, only enforcing them on you. The oversensitive conscience will feel guilty for not submitting to abuse. Misapplication of these ideas feed that undeserved guilt.

The idea of deserving abuse, understanding God's will, and the next section on sacrifice or suffering, are interrelated. Discussing them as threads in the complex web that makes paths in the abusive maze helps in sorting them out, since each one impacts another.

These are the same questions that have confronted thousands of earnest Christians who want to do God's will. Both the abused woman of faith and those who would help her have pain from feeling constrained by certain scriptures. Kroeger asks if we, like the legalists of Jesus' day, are misapplying the Scriptures. Jesus harshly challenged them when they enforced suffering.

> Carol Clark Kroeger writes about the inner turmoil woman of faith experience about helping abused women of faith. Her husband and she had come to a town to proclaim the Word of God. One bitter winter night, the abusive husband of a woman she was counseling was on the loose with and gun and was not afraid to use it. The terror in her heart was not because of the weather but because of her questions as a young pastor's wife: Had she stepped out of the will of God? Was she dishonoring the Lord by flouting what the Scriptures said about submission and the permanence of marriage? If she was disobedient, how could she expect God to help this woman who had already sustained such serious injuries at the hands of her husband? Would my efforts to save a life make a mockery of our ministry? What is the loving thing to do?

What is Enabling? Allowing the abuser to escape responsibility for his behavior in your relationship.

Peace at any price-you betray yourself to have peace but it increasingly does not work, You interpret this as failing as a peacemaker or wife.

Conspiracy of Silence-not talking about it or getting help lets him continue "take it to the Lord in prayer".

Getting you to Guilt-if you don't do it my way, you are the problem.

Your sense of duty-your kindness and sympathy mean no consequences for him; he gets to do what he wants freely.

Taking over responsibilities- frustration, easier to do it yourself, lets him off the hook.

Explaining it all away-all the excuses don't matter; he does it because it is working for him.

Recognize The 3 Goals of the Abuse

We are beginning to understand how the deliberate use of fear, guilt and shame help to maintain your partner's power and control over you. But what is the reason he wants that power and control?

By using "crazy-making" he <u>keeps you upset, doubting yourself and on edge</u>. This is called "gaslighting".

⊛Gaslighting

What is Gaslighting?

<u>Gaslighting</u> is a term used to describe an attempt to make a person question their reality. It is a conscious manipulation by someone else seeking control. That person suggests or outright claims that you should second-guess your reality. If someone is afraid to lose a relationship or disappoint an authority figure, they can be gaslighted.

If someone is taught not to recognize or trust their gut feelings, it is easier to suggest to her that she really doesn't think and feel the way she thinks she does. Some unethical leaders can gaslight by accusing our thoughts of being "faithless", our desires are "willful", our feelings are "worldly", all terms that can be used to argue them away. This makes it easier for the manipulator to control the person.

If a person protests or expresses feeling violated, the manipulator will argue it away. "Do you really feel that way?" "Why do you feel that way?" "Is it God's will for you to feel that way?" <u>Challenges to feelings should be a warning sign.</u> Feelings are a normal and natural part of living. They are not right or wrong. When the right to have an idea that differs is challenged, that is also a warning sign. A person may actually be told she didn't see what she saw. One minister threatened his wife with a knife while saying "You know I would never hurt you." This was meant to cause her to doubt what she was seeing and the fear she was feeling.

Not just the reality but the perception of the reality will be argued away. The person will be accused of lying, "bearing false witness", and other shaming phrases.

To cope with anyone who gaslights you, hold onto your truth. You only have one "you" and no one can replace you. Realize the gaslighter is getting a payoff of control by challenging you. He does not respect you and is not interested in your wellbeing. Realize he will not change by your explaining yourself. Detach and realize the motive for this behavior.

Because of faith ideals, you may believe that those who were vocal or seemed to be dedicated to your faith had the same motives as you did. You may have believed your husband's words when he said he wanted to build a new faith organization, or he was concerned to help you in your spiritual journey, or other ideal that you thought you both shared. You then entered into rationalizing or denying the reality of what was happening.

Finally, you come to face that he is getting everything he wants while accusing you of always disappointing him.

Margary realized this by charting his patterns. What did he do when she got money? How did he react when issues of sex arose? This showed that the patterns were consistent.

For example, Richard would storm off in the middle of the night and threaten to leave if she was tired and couldn't satisfy his sexual needs. He said he was a descendent of David, who had many wives. He should be allowed to have other women as well because of his dedication to the ministry.

Your charting will show what the "payoff" or benefit to him is for him. What does he get control or power over every time he uses the methods? Some men define manhood as controlling a woman, even if with violence. Other men just want the use of her body or permission to be with other women. Others want to access her money. And some want all three.

Here is where ideals may cloud your seeing what he is doing. Margary continued to believe they shared a desire to please God. From her experience, she stayed in her marriage too long because of her faith questions. She was brought up in the church and always had a strong relationship with Christ from a young girl on. She studied the Bible extensively.

She initially married Richard because he knew the Bible better than anyone she had met, was an eloquent preacher, a skilled leader, and was able to answer questions about the how faith worked in life. So when he, the churches, and society all said that she had to accept his use of God and her faith to create pain, she had work to do. Others without this background might have said, "This is crazy. I'm leaving." But she had to be clear about how her relationship with God was affected. It took a lot of work to accept that this was not God's will for her.

Define How the Stress of Coping Affects You

While she struggled with these questions, it added to her stress. While her relationship with God was helping her endure, she began to feel the effects of the constant pressure. The haranguing, conflicting expectations, accusations, and the other methods weakened her immune system.

Margary developed chronic demoralization, racing thoughts, sleep disturbances, irritable bowel syndrome, back problems, and depression. Margary was hospitalized finally from the broken ankle and shoulders when falling down the stairs after her husband deliberately tripped her. Her weakened state made it easier to harm her further.

In the past sections, we learned to use charting and labeling to sort through some of the badgering we have been subjected to that has taken a toll on our mental, emotional and spiritual health.

Now we will add a third tool, journaling, to expand and deepen our foundation. Adding this tool to charting and labeling completes the inner work tools. When we become more assertive, we know how to handle pressures that increase, not only from our partners, but also from others, perhaps including friends, family, faith community and others.

 *Tool Three: Cut Through the Maze with Journaling*

The idea of God's will is so important we will examine each of the ideas that you may be wrestling with. Harriet Lerner writes in *The Dance of Deception* "patriarchal injunctions promote silence and denial even about life-and-death matters, such as the horror and extent of male violence in women's lives." (p. 154)

The desire to be true to God's will can involves three beliefs. Examine them to see if these are being overemphasized as all-or nothing beliefs.

God's will is that I be willing to suffer or sacrifice.
God's will is that I be willing to forgive others when they hurt me.
God's will is striving to be like Christ, who died for us.

Suffering and Sacrifice

As a Christian, you believe in salvation through Christ. The question then is if you are already redeemed, why are you still being asked to suffer? Jesus said the kingdom of God is in you. Your body is a temple of the Holy Spirit. As a believer and even as a human being, **you, including your body, mind, heart and soul,** deserve respect. Suffering is as natural part of the physical life, but seeking unnecessary suffering is unhealthy.

There is no record of Jesus commanding women to be mistreated by their husbands. In fact, the record is that he rebuked those who would accuse and punish her.

It is not God's will that we continue to suffer by being with someone who is disobedient to God's desire for our abundant life. Jesus healed bodies. If your flesh is evil, why would Jesus show concern for its wellbeing?

We are made with free will. Only we can decide what we will believe and obey. Simply put, we can be free simply by not believing that we are being required to be in bondage.

Here are some major disconnects between the basis of how the abused and the abuser operate in the relationship. The more the victim tries to please, the more the abuser increases control.

She wants to please him.	He wants to control her.
She cannot believe he would deceive her.	He uses this belief to not be responsible.
She devotes her whole heart to him.	He feels unlimited power over her.
She believes what he says.	He tells her what she wants to hear.
She believes he only wants the best for her.	He tells her what he wants is the best for her.
She expects an honest answer to her questions.	He says she has no right to doubt him.
She wants to express herself.	He says she doesn't love him if she does.
She wants to explore her talents.	He says he should be enough for her.
She thinks if she can just make him understand, they can solve the problem.	He does understand and uses it against her.
She thinks if she can just make him realize she loves him, he will not be upset.	He is upset because he is not getting his way.

"The brain tends to freeze when threatened. This gives a sense of powerlessness." - Mike Phillips, pastor and therapist

We have the choice to stop believing the lies. One of the lies is that we must be abused to obey or please God as a Christian or wife. In many ways, the most surprising understanding Margary came to was that, when she thought she was being obedient, she actually was not. She had been misled about God's will for her as a Christian and wife.

What she had been told to do – submit to abuse– was not what God was telling her to do.

Forgiveness

_Jesus words about forgiving 70 x 7 are a favorite of abusers to keep from changing their behavior. The common understanding of this verse is that 70 x 7 means "unlimited". If Jesus said this, wouldn't that mean God forgives us as well?

Here we distinguish between forgiveness and forgetting. We forgive others to avoid holding hatred in our hearts, which separates us from God. In fact, that is one reason Margary had to leave the relationship. She could not continue to be misused and keep the peace in her heart she knew God wanted her to have. This was another indication that it was not God's will for her to be abused.

Forgiveness does not depend on the other person asking for it. However, it also does not mean continuing to be available for misuse. We need to heal and forgive to be healthy (whole) ourselves. Prisoners in concentration camps cannot

WHAT IS INTERMITTENT REINFORCEMENT?

The strongest kind of behavior conditioning is intermittent reinforcement. This type involves offering a reward or punishment for a behavior, but not every time.

For example, if you offer a treat if a child does what you want, that is positive reinforcement. If you punish him for doing something you don't want him to do, that is negative reinforcement.

But if he never knows when he will get a treat and only gets it once in a while, this is called intermittent reinforcement. It is the strongest way to condition behavior, because the child keeps hoping that this time he will get the treat.

If he gets a treat one time and a punishment the next time for the same behavior, this creates anxiety and confusion.

leave. Do you believe God wants you in a prison? Or is Christian history full of the opposite, Christians helping others escape? Jesus commanded us help the oppressed go free.

So it is not God's will that we stay in bondage, only that we get to the place where we can forgive. Jesus' idea of not striking back was radical. Certainly it did not mean a wife had to submit to an oppressive husband. The abuser hammers at verses which serve his purpose of control. But he exempts himself from obedience, forgiveness and sacrifice.

Dying

Dying for one's friend is a well-known verse. An abuser is not your friend. Helping does not mean saving. Saving an abuser is not our job. When Jesus died, it was a singular act and it was not at the hands of his partner. It was for us to have abundant life, not to pursue our own death. It is not God's will for us to suffer unto death in a marriage.

You know whether you are experiencing the fruits of the Spirit. You know what fruit the tree is bearing. Spiritual death is not the goal of the Christian life. You are free to decide if your spiritual life is healthy and growing or being suppressed and damaged. Only you know the effects of how you, and your children, if you have them, are being treated. But it is not a personal failure for you to not want to be constantly misused.

Each woman is responsible for her soul's wellbeing. It is tempting to want to escape this by "obeying" someone else but it is not an escape. You are still dealing with the effects of this decision. There is no advantage as you have been taught. Even a benevolent dictator is still a dictator.

We now see that the idea of "God's will" is used by those who want us to not challenge their desires, intentions, or actions. They are not concerned about doing God's will by honoring and loving their partner. Appealing to God's will is another no-win, deflecting or projecting tactic.

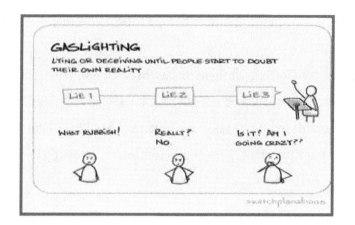

CHAPTER 4: EXERCISE

Chart or journal the ways your partner uses "God's will" to enforce your obedience, even against your faith. List ways he is practicing intermittent reinforcement.

1.   How does he use the idea of "God's will" to justify his methods, or the communication patterns of double bind, deflecting or projecting?_____

_____

2.   Does he use it to avoid responsibility, such as saying it's God's will he leave you and the children to go preach without providing for you yet forbidding you to work or have friends?

_____

_____

3.   Does he tend to say it's God's will when he wants to do something but not God's will if you want to do something similar?

_____

4.   Write about what your understanding of God's will has been up to this point.

_____

5. One verse says, "What does the Lord require of you but to do justice, love mercy and walk humbly with your God." Is this what predominates in your relationship now?

_____

_____

6. Are there ways you are trying to obey this but your partner is not? Is a one-way relationship God's will?

_____

_____

7. Love is one of the ideas that you may connect with God's will. You want to be loving. How is submitting to this abuse helping your partner be a loving person?

_____

8. How is the relationship draining your resources to be loving?_____

_____

9. Being like Christ is another idea you may connect with God's will. You believe Christ gave his life and said "No greater love has a man than to give his life for his friend." Do you believe you must give your life to this relationship?

_____

10. Is it God's will for you to allow your partner to destroy you? _____

_____

11. Notice the verse says "for his friend." Is your partner being friend?_____

_____

The abuse cycle is a classic example of intermittent reinforcement. A positive experience during the honeymoon phase is followed by negative experiences, followed by positive experiences again. The abuser will also alter positive and negative responses to the same behavior. For example, one meal he may criticize you for not cooking a certain food and another time ask why you don't make it because you should know it is his favorite. Have there been times this has happened to you?

_____

_____

11. Keep in mind that you are responsible for your own faith walk. No one can walk that for another person. You must work with the meaning of the Bible as much as your husband or anyone else. Those who advise you may be upholding male privilege, church interests, or other agendas rather than your welfare or Jesus' message. Has the idea of sacrifice been asked of you and not your partner? Do leaders ask you to not embarrass the church by seeking help?_____

_____

Write a letter explaining what you would say to someone using a Bible verse to justify hurting you. Use what you are learning to answer their objections to your desire to live as a Christian without being misused.

PRAYER

Dear Lord, I have felt and believed in your love for me. I know I have worth as your woman of faith. I now understand that there is no part of your will or plan for me that involves suffering at the hands of my partner, who took a vow to love and honor me. When one person breaks the contract, it is null and void. To keep my heart for you, I must stop accepting this abuse in your Name.

"When churches apply law to victims and grace to perpetrators, victims suffer while perpetrators celebrate. This is not love." Boz Tchividjian, **www.netgrace.org,2/8/18**

An apology means
nothing if they
don't stop doing
what they are
apologizing for.
Believe ACTION,
not words
—mandy hale

CHAPTER 5: DENIAL

MARGARY'S
STORY

If it wasn't God's will for me to suffer this way, there must be some other reason, some good that could come out of what I was going through.

I couldn't believe he was choosing to act this way. It could be that he had lost his way as a believer, and as his wife I needed to help him get back. Maybe I could help him.

We had been married some years when we visited a fellow minister's church. After service, the pastor and his wife invited us to lunch. Richard had a meeting and said I should go without him.

At the table they explained they had known my husband for many years. First they asked me how I came to meet him. Then, they approached me as if asking for my advice "since I was interested in ministry".

They described a young woman who was interested in church work being approached by an older minister, very articulate, handsome and charismatic "sort of like your husband" they said. They said he was showing an inappropriate interest in other women as well as this young woman. When she found out, they said, it broke her heart and jeopardized her faith for a while. "How would you advise her?" they asked me.

In deep denial about my husband's true character, I didn't take the hint.

"I think my husband has the most wisdom and experience in counseling people. I would send her to him. But if a wife does catch her husband being unfaithful, she should forgive him if he is sorry." I added.

"What if he has a child with another woman?" the pastor asked me.

"She should still forgive him. She shouldn't be like other women and be jealous. She should rise above that," I continued.

I didn't catch the look of disappointment on their faces, as they realized I was so deeply under his influence that I hadn't understood their warning.

Are you trying to save an abuser? Only God and the offending person can do that. Even God does not remove free will. Are you in denial about what you can do, even if you love him?

QUESTIONS

1. *Am I a failure as a believing wife?*
2. *Am I supposed to gladly bear persecution from my husband for my faith?*
3. *How is my subservience really helping him?*
4. *Is it my responsibility to fix every problem he creates?*
5. *Am I afraid to admit my faith can't save him?*

Margary had always coped with a "me and God" attitude. She believed Christ loved, protected and guided her. What she didn't realize was that some only used "Christian" as a way to manipulate her.

Richard was a master of labeling what was happening to his advantage. Wanting money from her relatives became "helped your family serve God." When he said he had left a church to seek advanced opportunities. she found out later he had been dismissed for misconduct. It was always someone else's fault.

Because he could be a model Christian, kind and helpful with others, Margary couldn't understand why he couldn't be reasonable at home. Even if it wasn't her fault, she thought there just must be something she needed to do to help him. She couldn't believe he would be deliberately misusing her.

She accepted his version of her experience. Trusting her own feelings and thoughts was condemned as faithless, sinful, or even wicked. He was using the Bible as a smokescreen to make his will dominant.

As her life became more and more chaotic, she increased her efforts to make it work. This meant denying that he was not a loving husband or, for that matter, a believer. Margary believed she was stronger and could single-handedly make it work when other women might not be able to.

Adding to her challenge was that church members, the pastor, friends and even family admired or praised her ability to be "longsuffering." They made comments like "She's such a saint." Not only did she not want to disappoint or displease her husband, she also wanted to uphold her status in the community and not disappoint others. On the other hand, those who believed his image had difficulty believing her if she sought help. Margary thought if she just tried harder, she could salvage her marriage. No matter how many promises he broke, she made an excuse for him. He would say he repented, even go to counseling, but when he thought he was past the point of being held responsible, he would go back to his pattern: create a problem, blame her but keep her depending on him.

LEVEL 4 – You Know It's Not God's Will but You Still Want to Help Him

Faith Concept: Sacrifice as Love

In this chapter, you will….

>*Evaluate the unsound assumptions that are holding you back*
>*Identify why your previous attempts to help him have not worked*
>*Face the extent of the damage you have suffered*
>*Break the denial*

The manipulating skills of the abuser allow him to always have an answer for why your concerns are not valid, projecting his faults on you, and avoiding taking responsibility for his part in the relationship with a complete set of smokescreen tools. You have now had enough experience to recognize these behaviors, but you are concerned that you as a believer have a responsibility to try to help your partner come away from these damaging and hostile practices.

It takes a special kind of person to want to help someone who has misused them so badly. What would account for this lack of self-defense, even survival instinct, in a woman?

It is hard to admit we cannot help someone we care about. Our pride in being a good person is struck; our desire to be successful in a faithful life is challenged. We must redefine our definition of relationship, faith, love and giving to remove unreasonable expectations. God placed free will in us. Your partner is making the decision to not be a faithful loving partner. God is allowing this. You however have a responsibility to witness that this is not the will of God for married couples or for you. Use your journal to explore the following tasks.

Evaluate the Unsound Assumptions That Are Holding You Back

Women may tend to see the success of relationships as their primary work. In some ways, women are made for love. That is why, in my view, women are more drawn to spiritual life. From a little girl on, we learn to anticipate other's needs, to try to make them happy, to cheer them up when they are low, to feed them, make them comfortable, and support them in every way. This is part of the Christian message, care for others. Our lives are directed toward others: we are children of parents, then wives of husbands, and then mothers of children. Even busy professional women still deal with the relationships as important parts of their happiness.

So we are used to putting ourselves second. We sacrifice for others almost second nature. Even if we know his behavior toward us is not our fault, our nature as women as well as our belief system tells to return good for evil, kindness for cruelty, forgiveness for pain. We forget the second part of the Great Commandment, to love others as ourselves.

When does this become a problem? Because a narcissistic or abusive person misuses that belief as an open door and permission to abuse us further. Basically we have to accept that an abuser is not operating on the same basis as we are.
If nothing else is clear from what we have suffered, we see that what we have done to try to make it work has not worked. Trying just keeps us stuck in his game. The abuser does not value Christian love, kindness, the marriage vow, or a healthy partnership. It

is hard to admit that someone we love is not interested in our welfare. We tend to believe that if we can just make him understand, he will stop. We find it hard to believe he does understand and is hurting us deliberately. As Sally Compton said, "It is hard to fight an enemy whose outpost is in your head."

Many forms of abuse are criminal but not discussed honestly. Some of us were physically restrained. Our habeas corpus rights were violated. In the past, wives were not allowed to bring charges against their husband's assaults. It was not even called assault because it happened in the woman's home and not on the street. Men have been excused with minimizing expressions like "he must have had a bad day" "what did she say to upset him" or "he has a temper problem".

Here are some helpful phrase patterns for when you are trying to clarify or reveal the unspoken assumption or accusation.

Are you trying to….or…	Are you trying to insult me or just not thinking about what you are saying?
Let me say if you…you might…	Let me say if you didn't shout, I might be able to hear what you are saying.
What is it about….that	What is it about not vacuuming that makes me lazy?
You mean it's….if I don't (or do)….	You mean it's stupid if I disagree with you?
If you…then I… Or If…then…	If you cannot stop screaming, then I will have to leave until you can talk to me reasonably.
Just because….doesn't mean….	Just because I didn't have dinner ready doesn't mean I'm a derelict wife.

Identify Why You Cannot Help Him

In the book, _Is It Love or Addiction_ by Brenda Schaeffer, the reader can see how they have mislabeled as love an unhealthy relationship of codependency, an addictive relationship, or traumatic bonding. There is no shame in this. It is a way some are taught to relate. But it is full of pain and we want to leave this pain so we can have healthy relationships and practice our faith and heart connection with God.

Codependent styles of relating are learned in childhood or even confused with what it means to relate as Christians. Our happiness is dictated by the emotional state of the other person. We are taught that we are responsible for the happiness of others. This is not reality but is our way of relating until we learn better.

To help a person, there must be a foundation of respect. The person must honor the helper as someone who has what will benefit them. However abusers want to use the helper's benefits but not to improve or grow or heal. They want to use them because it makes them feel powerful and in control. Any help from the person that does not result in more power and control will be rejected.

See the inset explaining Emotional Vampires and Emotional Blackmailers. These persons' behaviors range from mild personality disorders to sadism.

We have all seen times when, because of emotional history or issues, the very person who wants to help is the person who cannot. Parents have experienced this with children for example. Even with interventions, the person has to want to change for any long- term healing.

We may have cherished the ideal that a truly great spiritual person can save someone in spite of themselves. That would make us feel very proud if we could do that. However lifeguards have special techniques to do this. The lifeguard is saving someone who is helpless. Your partner is not helpless. He is trying to keep you helpless. Imagine a lifeguard trying to rescue someone who is stabbing them. That is your situation. This is not the example of Jesus. Jesus would heal people by their faith, their willingness to be healed. By dying on the cross, Jesus allowed himself to be subject to his persecutors for a specific, one- time purpose. <u>He did not stay subjugated in the name of</u> <u>saving anyone</u>.

He resisted those who would misuse him the rest of the time. He refused to give in to temptations of controlling others, attempts to trick him, and misuse of his powers. He did not cooperate with those who sought to demean him. This is being Christ-like rather than thinking we can take the place of Christ's power in our abuser's life. <u>Your partner does not respect you</u>. If he did he would not be abusing you. You have no responsibility to try to help him because he is not open to help from you. What about "the prayer of the faithful avails much"? This is true but you can pray for him and still be out of reach for harmful behavior. Continuing to accept or be available for abuse, even if verbal, does nothing but encourage him to continue to think he has access to someone who will accept mistreatment. This is codependent behavior. For mothers, we have to ask ourselves if we have the right to continue to subject your children to this harm? What is that doing for their faith?

> There's always
> a little truth behind every
> "just kidding,"
> a little knowledge behind every
> "I don't know,"
> a little emotion behind every
> "I don't care,"
> and a little pain behind every
> "It's okay."

Face the Extent of the Damage You Have Suffered

If your relationship is an addictive one, it means you feel as if you cannot survive without the other person. Both of these styles, codependency and addiction, are learned early and are very damaging. Margary's husband felt no guilt or remorse for lying to his wife about his affair, but she was afraid to confront him and became increasingly ill. Relationships in which there is an imbalance in the amount of responsibility for the relationship often may result in the more empathetic and responsible member becoming ill. She was not being honest with herself or her partner, and her immune system was compromised.

By trying to "help" him, we are confusing "help" with being over-responsible. The more we do, the less he does to create peace, harmony, and love.

In fact we see that he is glad to shift the blame to us for any of the negative consequences of his behavior. We learned this is called projection. Like the hot potato game, we can stop the pain by not catching his emotional hot potato. Good boundaries create safe harbors in which to change, to heal and to grow. Boundaries are the first sign of the journey from denial into honesty.

Break the Denial

We have to ask ourselves why we think we should accept this treatment but not hold our partners to the same standards. Do we think we are more spiritual? better? have a higher calling? Or simply accepting other's teachings that we don't have the right to be treated with love and respect by our partners and to leave if they have broken the vow. Why are some "Christians" intent on preventing us from escaping this treatment? Why do they support the abuser's cause but not ours? We must begin to question and not blindly accept other's versions of what our faith should be so we can mature in our relationship with God. Facing reality is not being faithless.

We may be concerned when others say, "Well, he may not be a good husband but he is a good father." No man who mistreats his wife, the mother of his children, is being a good father. The children see and are harmed by what they see, the tension in the home, and the disrespect of their mother affects them throughout their lives. It creates issues for their future relationships, whether they are boys or girls.

We now understand that we have been trying to do what only God can do. We have been exhausting ourselves trying to do what we should not be trying to do because we did not understand and were encouraged to do so by others. However we see now that God is not blessing our efforts.

We now understand that God does not want us to be abused. We didn't know we were being misled. Setting our husbands between us and God almost led us into idolatry. No one has the right to treat us this way. It is not pleasing to God and we should not comply with it.

We need to honor ourselves as God's creation. God is not answering our prayers to change the abuser because that is not our job. We are to let go and let God, releasing our partner to his own free will and spiritual development. We must leave him to God and work out our own spiritual development by abiding in love ourselves. This means shunning the evil of abuse and moving "from grace to grace."

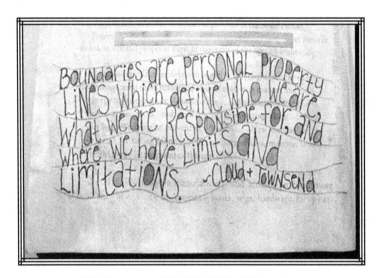

Unknown CC-BY-NA-SA

Emotional Blackmailers and Emotional Vampires

Be aware of two approaches to misusing your emotions. One is emotional blackmail and the other is behaving as an emotional vampire.

Emotional Blackmail is a phrase used to describe those who uses your caring against you. They know you take pride in being a caring person. They use this desire to get what they want but if you ask for consideration for what you did for them, they instill guilt.

For example, one woman's husband would complain of a need, she would offer to take care of it (loan money, take him to an interview, etc.). Then when she needed some consideration and he refused, she would say, "But I helped you when you needed it" whereupon he would say "I didn't ask you to."

I am always reminded of Lucy in the Peanuts cartoon. No matter how many times Lucy promises not to pull the football away as Charlie goes to kick it, she always does. Sometimes called "trust bandits", these people take advantage of your hope that this time it will be different.

Emotional blackmailers first convince you that no one should do anything to upset them. Then when they get upset over any trivial matter, which is inevitable, they will make you feel it is your fault.

Of they will encourage you to do something against your will and then abandon you if you are exposed for doing it. Patty Hearst and other captives are well known examples. In other words, they get you to do their dirty work for them and try to keep you in control by blaming you.

Emotional vampires drain you of your emotional strength. They take all of your caring until you are empty. They then move on to a fresh person to drain. Women who are afraid of being abandoned or rejected, who fear displeasing or disappointing anyone or who blame themselves if this happens, are prime sources for emotional vampires.

Some Bible verses are misused to encourage a woman to continue this devastating and deadening approach to having a relationship. For example, Margary donated her salary to her husband's mission work. When she needed a new pair of shoes, her husband accused her of being selfish and misusing the money that "The Lord" had given her the ability to earn and which should all be used for "the work". Margary felt she did not have permission to have any needs at all.

These two toxic attacks on your emotional health stir up your emotions, push your buttons and throw you off center. Empaths, or people who are highly sensitive to other people's emotional state or who are highly compassionate, suffer the most around this type of person.

People-pleasing, lack of assertive skills, depression or low self-esteem, fatigue, or overwhelming responsibilities can create more susceptibility to this toxic manipulation.

CHAPTER FIVE: EXERCISE

Use your journal to face the extent of your damage:

<u>Physical:</u> Are you beginning to have worsening physical problems? Check any that apply.

Shortness of breath	Heart palpitations	Chest pain	Sweating
Chills	Choking	Dizziness	Trembling
Nausea	Diarrhea	Numbness	Disorientation
Fear of going crazy	Fear of losing control	Fear of dying	Neglecting health
Recklessness	Forgetting	Hysteria	Uncontrolled crying

<u>Emotional:</u> Are you finding it harder and harder to function normally?

_____

Do small mishaps bring you to tears?

_____

Do you find that rage rushes to your chest unexpectedly? This is called "emotional lability" or "emotional instability" and is the result of the constant stress you are under. Your abuser will be happy to condemn you for it after creating it,

_____

_____

List your experiences which would show you are being used by an emotional blackmailer. Do you have a pattern of offering help without being asked?_____

Mental: Do you find that the effort to think clearly is becoming harder?_____

Does your mind feel numb at times_____

Do you find it difficult to remember things that used to be easy for you? Are you making more simple mistakes?

_____

_____

_____

Spiritual: Are you struggling to know how to please God when you cannot please your husband? _____

Are your faith leaders placing the blame for your trials on your lack of faith or obedience? _____

Are they encouraging you to accept abuse in the name of your salvation?

_____

Are you wondering how God can allow you to suffer like this when you want to do good? _____

Do you find it harder to make sense of what your experience of your loving God is with what you are living now?_____

Are you forbidden to or shamed if you question or discuss your faith challenges?

_____

Do you want to have love in your heart but find that the constant harassment is making I difficult?

_____

_____

Assumptions: What have been some misgivings or ideas that have held you back?_____

_____

Why you cannot help him: Review what you now understand about why he is beyond your ability to change him._____

_____

Break the denial: Describe what you now realize you were denying.

_____

_____

Letter to Those Who Would Discourage Me or Keep Me In Bondage:

_____

_____

_____

_____

My Prayer: "Dear God, I cannot help him because he does not respect me. It does not help him to allow him to abuse me. He must take his spiritual journey and I must take mine. I now see more clearly how I must stay with you on my spiritual journey. I am ready to stop believing in my lesser spiritual status. I am sorry I believed this was part of your kingdom. I release my abuser to you. He must become willing to open his heart and mind to your Holy Spirit. I must trust You and begin to live in your love and dignity. Please continue to strengthen me to not accept the attacks of him who would 'accuse your people night and day before you.' Amen. "

"The painful reality that clergy are involved in criminal activity can no longer be ignored and protocol is urgently needed in response to these acts where ...violence ... is perpetrated against clergy wives and children," -The Pastoral Report to the Churches on Sexual Violence Against Women and Children in the Church Community. 1990 in collaboration with the Catholic Church, Anglican Church, Churches of Christ, Uniting Church and Salvation Army.

"Spiritual abuse is not caused by a wrong understanding of Scripture." Karen Wilson, Recovery from Spiritual Abuse. 1karenwilson.weebly.com

CHAPTER 6: DESPAIR

I had spent years rationalizing, minimizing, or avoiding reality to justify his behavior. Now an overwhelming despair engulfed me. It had all been a lie.

When he maxed out my credit cards, I thought I could just get him to stop. When he poured poison in my bathroom drinking cup to teach me "to watch your mouth", I thought I could bear it. When he stood over me on the floor, cursing when my back went out, I drew further within, determined to survive.

When my health sank so far I was hospitalized, I had to admit he knew what he was doing. He knew he was using my faith to hurt me. He had no interest in changing. I had devoted myself to an abuser.

Sorrow weakened my spirit. At these times, I repeated the lyrics to comforting hymns, "Be Still My Soul" and "Guide Me, Oh You Great Jehovah". After hours of rebukes, I choked on sobs and could not answer him. I was a nervous wreck and mentally tormented. I couldn't think of realistic options. The dread in my gut spread throughout my body. I feared there was no hope as a believer, a wife, and a woman.

My family could not help. He had insulted friends. I was ashamed to go to the neighbors. I certainly couldn't go to members of our church. As a community leader, I didn't want to go to a shelter run by the same women I had been on committees with.

Gradually I turned more into myself. Holding my feelings inside on the roller coaster made me sicker. Eventually I was in total despair. I began imagining how I might kill myself. Would I run the car into a tree? Could I swallow enough pills? But I couldn't leave my children with him.

One day driving home from work, I couldn't keep going. I physically could not make myself go home. I pulled to the side of the road and put my head down on the steering wheel. As I waited, cars continued to whizz past me. Finally, a policeman pulled up behind me and came to my car. "Lady, are you all right?" he asked. The look on my face must have given him the answer. But I couldn't face making Richard angrier by getting a cop involved. I gathered myself together and told him I was just checking a map. He went back to his car.

I realized if I had to lie to a policeman, my situation had reached the point where I had to act. I couldn't continue this way.

Have you reached the end?

QUESTIONS:

1. *What is keeping you from facing the despair?*
2. *What are you telling yourself about why you should continue this way?*
3. *How long do you think you can go on?*
4. *Which fear is worse? fear of people knowing, of nowhere to go, admitting you can't make it work, or of his anger?*
5. *Is it the confusion, the not knowing what to do, that is holding you back?*

In this chapter, you will…

Recognize effects of shock, exhaustion and other stressors
Learn your assertive rights as a believer
Defend yourself mentally with affirmations
Practice assertive communication

Because her faith was so strong, Margary wanted to get guidance from God on what to do. She had taken a vow and was not going to break it lightly. She was not as concerned for herself as much as for her children. She began to see the damage Richard's abuse was doing to them. She realized that she would be to blame if she didn't help them.

The constant, escalating pressures of living with an abusive person takes its toll on your entire being at every level. You feel despair because of the damage at four layers: denying what is going on, condemning your thoughts, numbing your feelings, and finally admitting you can't win.

In Level 1, you processed the first layer of damage. You have avoided as much as you can, minimized and made excuses for his behavior.

When you deny or repress normal anger, you then began to feel fragmented, as what you believed about your relationship comes into conflict with the way it is. At this point, your body's nervous and other systems go into survival mode. This involves numbing as outlets for normal feelings are blocked. Since everyone has a normal range of feelings, condemning them is really a tactic to keep you feeling guilty and controllable.

In numbing you begin to separate from yourself and you find thinking increasingly difficult. You may feel actual physical fuzziness or dullness in and around your brain. Your thinking, your ability to recognize what is going on and function or respond becomes impaired. A common sign of excessive stress is making simple mistakes, forgetting things you used to know, not being able to drive routes you used to, and the like. Of course, the abuser is ready to pounce on you to upbraid you even more for these mistakes. Other illnesses may activate: autoimmune related, depression, anxiety, irritable bowel syndrome, vision problems, headaches and other stress activated conditions.

At the fourth level are the effects of trying to cope for so long. This is the desire to fix him. You try unsuccessfully to avoid his baiting or triggering you and instead you focus on healing him. Here is where most of us tried different ways to communicate. We now want to explore assertive communications as part of this level. This will show you clearly that he will not respond to a reasonable pattern of interaction in a relationship. What he means by "good communication" from you is limited to "yes, dear" "right away, dear". And even that won't stop the attacks.

When you can't fix him, you feel despair because you feel powerless and trapped.

This is the turning point where there is hope!
If you don't deny it, God's life begins to well up in you again.
You begin to know deep within you that this is not right.
The resentment that your bondage creates is one evidence it is not God's will for
you to accept it.

Resentment is frozen, unexpressed feelings of being mistreated. At this point many tell a woman to confess her sin. "Be ye angry and sin not." If you honor these feelings and don't deny them, you can use their energy to help you. Getting angry is a good sign. It means you are coming out of despair. Anger is the normal response to being violated. Telling you to not be angry is just another weapon to keep you trapped.

Your anger is your body's self -defense response. It calls your attention to what needs to be addressed. It is not sinful in these cases. Jesus showed anger when people were misused by others. Your abuser, on the other hand, uses anger aggressively and abusively to deny your right to protect yourself after hurting you.

We have all used unhealthy or inappropriate ways to deal with our anger. | ✓*yes!* Living with a raging person can make us even more afraid of examining our own anger. Some futile approaches to managing or expressing anger are blocking it, delaying it, freezing it, twisting it, repressing it, turning it against ourselves, turning it on others, or sugar-coating it. The healthy way to use our anger is to examine the situation and beliefs, recognize what has been violated, and choose a way to turn the energy toward our well-being. All feelings have physical energy that has to be channeled in positive ways or they can come out in harmful but unrecognized ways. The unhappy "helper" who tries to control others is perhaps the classic example.

✂ *Tool 5- Cut Through the Maze with Assertive Communication*

The three most powerful types of assertions are positive, personal rights, and negative assertions. Positive assertions state your position, personal rights assertions state your boundaries, and negative assertions state what you will not participate in or tolerate. *3 assertive ways to communicate*
Write an example of each one now:

Positive assertion:_____

Personal right assertion:_____

Negative assertion: _____

Practicing Defending Yourself Mentally with Affirmations

Because of the dangerous situation you are in, you need to break the despair. Draw now upon the energy of your anger. Instead of screaming and crying, however, you will channel it into honoring your voice. The more you practice, the stronger you will get.

Strengthening your mind against his attacks was the first step. You developed your convictions through labeling and journaling. You found some words to use. The main ways in this workbook help you begin to counter the destructive messages and treatment you have received. They develop a foundation that keeps you from accepting abuse or returning to the abuser should it become necessary to leave.

> Keep a journal to address your questions and affirm God's love for you daily.
> Seek support from those who believe in you.
> Use affirmations to help rebuild your sense of self-worth.
> Learn and rehearse assertive communication aloud

At this point in your work, it is not time to directly challenge the abuser because he will escalate the abuse. You must first repair the inner damage to your self-worth to rebuild the foundation so you can withstand the attacks. In this chapter we learn to practice standing up for ourselves mentally and verbally. If he doesn't change, these skills strengthen you against pressures to go back to abuse if you have to leave.

Review the unsound assumptions you uncovered in the last chapter. We want to build a truer, stronger set of operating ideas. While many of us cling to comforting Bible verses like those in the Psalms and Jesus' love, it is also important to put our needs into our own words. Rehearsing affirming statements first mentally and then aloud strengthens and empowers us. There is power in the spoken word. Here are some helpful examples to maintain stability and strength when countering attacks:

"I am focusing on what I can control, the present moment."
"In this present moment, I focus on my breath."
"I control my attention, noticing what is going on but not taking it on."
"I am feeling…. and it is normal to feel this way."
"The only thing I need to do in this situation is…."
"I have a choice of what I believe."
"I am not responsible for another's desire to hurt someone."
"I choose to act in a way that lessens harm to myself."
"I make mistakes but am a worthwhile woman."
"I am a caring, loving, helpful woman."
"I am a responsible, competent woman."
"I am a beneficial presence in this world."
"God loves me and so do I."
"I can be anxious and still deal with this situation."

"I can take my time, let go and relax."
"I feel and do not judge my feelings."

Next, we learn and practice aloud assertive communication by ourselves and with a supportive person. We simply explain our boundaries. We are not blaming the other person. We are taking care of our "side of the street", taking responsibility for our own well-being. That is why sometimes phrases like "The Lord rebuke you" are not assertive. This type of statement will create even more backlash from the abuser. Margary's husband said she had no right to correct him and that The Lord would rebuke her for saying it, striking her as part of "Christian domestic discipline.

Assertive communication focuses on expressing our own needs, boundaries and intentions. It is not "tit for tat". We ignore those who condemn us for being honest with ourselves. We express our needs and allow the other person his views without insulting the other person. We practice the courage to speak them. We stop being silenced. Quivering, trying to please him, cowering, at the expense of our relationship with God and ourselves is over.

Rehearsing Assertive Responses Aloud

All three types of assertions use what is called "the data", how it affects you, what you want in the relationship and what you intend to do. The "data" is the observable or measurable facts that cannot be disputed, such as a door slamming.
Example: "Slamming the door upsets me. Please stop slamming the door." ✳ *gives examples which is very helpful*

Two inflammatory words to avoid are "you" and "why". Instead of "you never" stay with the observable data: "I haven't been out of the house for a week." Instead of "why" or "why didn't you (call like you said you would)" (a double whammy), say "I expected your call last night".

The next step is to explain what you will do.
Example: " Slamming the door upsets me. If you keep slamming the door, I will go to the library until you calm down."

It is very important not to express an intention if you are not going to do it. Every time you say you are going to leave, for example, and don't leave, you are weakening your position and encouraging him to not take you seriously.

When you begin being assertive, he may turn on the tears, playing a helpless victim. He will pretend to be hurt at your lack of caring. But when this doesn't work, he will cycle back into aggression to increase control.

Your partner is not interested in healing the relationship. He enjoys upsetting you. He does not care what you want. Identify the payoff. Margary's husband admitted to her that he enjoyed getting her upset. When she learned that, she stopped being upset, learned to detach, and began turning her attention to taking care of herself. He did not change other hurtful behaviors, but he did stop trying to goad her into a screaming match.

Someone who cares about you is not triggered into abuse by assertive communication. A manipulator will act offended because you are resisting his control. It is an act because when it doesn't work, he switches it. It was a ploy to make you feel guilty. He wants you to keep feeling responsible for his behavior. You know this now and no longer buy into this game.

In your charting, labeling and journaling, you got to the place where you know what the pressures will be to bring you back under abusive control. You have more power and control now you can withstand these toxic tactics.

Once you begin to stand up for yourself and stop cooperating in your destruction, the abuser will get more abusive if switching tactics doesn't work. Before you begin to assert yourself, make some plans on what to do and stand fast in your truth. Tell those who support you to know and be prepared. Some women have a recorder or camera running. At the later stages, it may not be possible to talk at all.

The Believing Woman's Spiritual Bill of Rights

The right to your personal relationship with God. I Peter 1:8

The right to discover your own beliefs and faith journey. Mark 2:26

The right to use the talents and gifts God gave you. Mark 4:21

The right to honor your body. II Cor 6:16

The right to follow the "still small voice of God". John 10:4

The right to separate from disrespectful relationships. Matt 10:14

The right to disagree. Matt 10:20

The right to friendships. Mark 3:35

The right to live in spiritual equality. John 5:24

An Assertive Bill of Rights

Physical:

- Not to be pushed, shoved, pounded, slapped, bruised, kicked or strangled. Not for any reason, not because of alcohol, unemployment, money problems, sickness, children, stress or religion
- Not to be attacked verbally, false accusations, name calling, yelling, lying or your reality denied
- Not to have possessions damaged (You are not one of his possessions)
- Not to be interfered with in coming and going
- Not to be followed, harassed, spied on
- Not to be isolated, but to have your privacy and independence respected

Verbal:

- The right to ask for what we want (realizing that the other person has the right to say "No")
- The right to have an opinion, feelings and emotions and to express them appropriately.

- The right to say I don't know, I don't understand, or I don't care.
- The right to offer no reasons or excuses for justifying your behavior.
- Not to be ridiculed, put down, made fun of,

Mental:

- The right to judge your own behavior, thoughts and emotions.
- The right to judge whether you are responsible for finding solutions to other's problems.
- The right to make illogical decisions
- The right to make our own decisions and to cope with the consequences.
- The right to choose whether to get involved with the problems of someone else.
- The right to know about something, or to understand.
- The right to make mistakes and be responsible for them.
- The right to change our mind.

Emotional:

- The right to change ourselves and be assertive people.
- The right to be successful.
- Not to be emotionally starved
-

Here are the guidelines on how to deliver an assertive response:

Actual Words – 7%
The way words are delivered (tone, accents on certain words, etc.) – 38%
Facial expressions – 55%

<u>Voice</u>

use a strong, confident voice*
be direct, without using hints, excuses, and/or apologies.
make statements, rather than asking questions.
speak slowly and directly to the person

Statements

use "I" to say how you are feeling and affected without judgement or blaming
name the specific behavior (do not use sarcasm, accusations, labels or
assumptions)
use "broken record", repeating the same statement 3-4 times before trying
another method
use "No" repeatedly.
feel free to interrupt by saying "I'm going to have to interrupt you." to stop the
words (listening gives the impression you are interested or willing to be
involved or subject to verbal abuse)
ignoring – when abuse is a "parting shot" or other inflammatory statement, not
responding can de-escalate, depending on the situation. Sometimes focusing on
the "payoff" is as successful as words.

Confident Body Language

Stand with planted feet
Keep your shoulders back and your hands available
Look at the person

Using assertive communication is a necessary bridge we must cross. Of course, if
we had known then what we know now, we would have stood up earlier and avoided
this heartache, since he would have either respected us or moved on. Sometimes the new
assertive behavior will get your partner's attention and, if he values his relationship with
you, he might begin to look within himself and seek help. Unfortunately, many do not.
But either way, you must learn to speak and act confidently and assertively to reclaim
your strength to deal with moving forward.

*practice even if your voice shakes. Keep at it and you will speak more firmly.

Letter to My Inner Spirit:

_____

_____

_____

My Prayer: "Dear God, I realize I was misled in thinking that I would be able to change or help without his consent. You give us free will. We cannot take that away. We can only take care of our side of the street. I now realize it does not help him to be able to abuse me. It is not good for either one of us. I need to be honest about my thoughts and feelings. I need courage to speak my truth despite attack. I need to be me as you gave me my one life, uniquely mine. I am growing in honoring that life. Continue to strengthen me. Thank you. Amen."

"'Spiritual homelessness' names the internal displacement that many abuse survivors experience." Dr, Denise Starkey, *Survivors' Faith Journeys*, Faith Trust Institute, June 15, 2016

Its not about him though...

CHAPTER SIX: EXERCISE

Journaling: Use your journal to try writing what an assertive response would be to the verbally abusive statements. Find someone to practice these aloud with role play if possible.

1. **Abuse Disguised as a Joke and denial of it**
   Example: "Jesus would have been up a creek with you helping him."
   Possible Responses: "The way you talk to me is insulting."
   (directly address the intent)

   His statement:
   Your Response:

---

2. **Withholding and Deprivation (refusing touch, affection, information, compliments, conversation or more)**
   Example: "I can't be yoked with an unbeliever." (As an excuse to not interact with you.)
   Possible responses: "That's good to know." (unexpected response; throws him off)

His statement: _____

Your response: _____

3. Countering:

Example: "You are to keep silent."

Possible responses: "Jesus conversed with women."

(use a direct reasonable fact)

His statement:_____

Your Response:_____

4. Discounting (denying your perceptions so don't have to take responsibility) Example:

"You must be confused. I would never do that. Why are you falsely accusing me?"

Possible Response: "I did not see you last night."

(staying with the observable behavior reduces defensiveness)

His

statement:_____

Your

Response:_____

5. Blocking and Diverting

Example: "You are to be angry and sin not." (to keep you from expressing resistance to mistreatment).

Possible Response: "Anger is a normal response to being falsely accused."

(affirm your right to be human) is statement:_____

Your Response:

WHEN A TOXIC PERSON CAN NO LONGER CONTROL YOU, THEY WILL TRY TO CONTROL HOW OTHERS SEE YOU. THE MISINFORMATION WILL FEEL UNFAIR, BUT STAY ABOVE IT, TRUSTING THAT OTHER PEOPLE WILL EVENTUALLY SEE THE TRUTH, JUST LIKE YOU DID.

Jill Blakeway

6. Accusation and Blame Example: "If you would give me a break, I wouldn't have to be upset all the time." Possible Response: "I am your partner and deserve consideration." (identify the underlying expectation, presumption or accusation)

His statement:_____

Your Response:_____

7. Judging and Criticizing
   Example: "My secretary understands me better than you and she's new."
   Possible Response: "She sounds like a good secretary."
   (refuse to be diminished or hurt)

   His statement:_____

   Your Response: _____

8. Trivializing and undermining
   Example: "You couldn't have got that scholarship if I hadn't watched the kids for you."
   (they are both your kids)
   Possible Response: "That's right. I would have had to hire a babysitter." (refuse to be baited)

   His statement: _____

   Your Response:_____

9. Name Calling
   Example: "You're a daughter of Satan."
   Possible Response: "I don't like being falsely accused."
   (refuse the insult)

   His statement: _____

   Possible Response: _____

10. Ordering and Demanding
   Example: "Pick up my cleaning and don't let dinner be late or else.!"
   Possible Response: "I couldn't hear what you said," or "Did you ask me if I had time to do that?" or "Did you say you were picking up dinner?" or "I don't think I heard you ask what I was doing today." "I don't cooperate with threats." Or other tactic that shows he is not speaking to you in a commonly courteous way.
   (refuse to respond to or comply with being rudely spoken to)

His statement:_____

Your Response:_____

11. Deliberate Forgetting or Denial

Example: "You can't expect me to remember everything with all the stress I have."

Possible Response: "Certainly not. I merely asked you what you said to me earlier this morning."

(reduce the general to the specific)

His statement:_____

Your Response:_____

12. Abusive Anger

Example: "You think this is angry? You'll know when I'm ANGRY!"

Possible Response: "Yes I do. And I am no longer subject to it."

(refuse to be intimidated or allow denial)

His statement:_____

Your Response:_____

13. Threatening Words

Example: "If you leave, I will kill you and the children."

Possible Response: "The more you threaten, the less I want to stay."

(do not reward the negative attempt by complying)

His statement:_____

Your Response:_____

(✳) **Threatening behavior should be reason to remove yourself and any children immediately.**

Now you have made some plans on how to address the most common verbal abuses he uses. Practice them and others when you are alone in front of a mirror or role play with a friend. Writing them out repeatedly also helps keep you stable when you are in a heated exchange with him.

It only it was that simple.

CHAPTER 7: DETERMINATION

MARGARY'S
STORY

Emerging from the despair was the hardest hurdle.

My faith in God had not waivered, but I had bought serious errors about what God wanted for me. I saw how I had been deliberately misled; I got angry. And I allowed myself this anger. I didn't argue it away. I didn't "repent" because it was not sinful to be angry about being abused. The abuse is the sin. Instead I used it to fuel my determination. I would regain my dignity as a believer. I would listen to Christ within me rather than those who would hurt me in God's name.

He would promise to repent, get counseling or change. Then it would all start again, only worse. When he promised to go to counseling, I came back. That was a mistake. He just felt stronger and took his campaign to women of the church, accusing me of disobedience. They began shunning me. Choir women began offering their shoulders for him to cry on. They chose the minister instead of supporting a hurting woman. Perhaps it would be scary to admit they had believed or supported a fraud. Or they might have thought "It could be me". Or maybe I was a mirror.

A major pattern was pretending to change until he thought he had won. He would Slandering me behind the scenes broadened to the church. He revealed private details about our life in his sermons, warning men to be wary of their wives leading them astray. Or warning women to submit or go to hell. Everyone knew he was condemning me to the church. He justified hitting me with "smite a scorner" or "whom He loves He chastises". "Count it all joy when you are tried" only applied to his trying me. There was no low below where he would go.

Each day I had a goal of trying to keep some violence from breaking out. I always failed. Everything was always inside out, upside down and bent backwards. If a woman bends backwards far enough, she is going to fall down. And he was glad when I was down. He wasn't going to stop. I would have to stop it.

I learned to face what was happening, what he was doing, not what he said. Those who have not experienced manipulators do not understand that they accuse others of what is true of them. He had proved he wouldn't get help. I did not have the right to ask my children to go through this damage. "Obeying my husband" would not hold up in court if I did not protect them.

He constantly threatened to kill me if I left. When I tried to call 911, he said he would cut me up in little pieces before the police arrived. We ran across the street to a neighbor's, while he chased us screaming "I'll kill you, whore of Babylon!". This was from a man who had two denominational ordinations.

If I believed in Christ, it meant I deserved respect. It meant I could be there for my children if I was there for myself. I began to pray about how to get out and make it on my own.

Are you determined to follow Christ into freedom?

QUESTIONS

1.   *What have I lost or gained so far by trying to keep the marriage together?*
2.   *What will likely happen if I continue with a man working against God's will?*
3.   *Are there conditions when God forgives breaking a marriage vow?*
4.   *I hate to admit I have failed. Am I being prideful to continue?*

LEVEL 5 OBJECTIVES – You Are Clear You Cannot Help Him But You Don't Know Whether You Should Stay

Faith Concept: Freedom

<u>In this chapter you will…</u>

> *Identify your top misgivings about leaving*
> *Review the four qualities of the spiritually healthy relationship*
> *Recognize the invalid pressures to stay*
> *Define your bottom line*
> *Claim your rewards for releasing him to God*

Margary was not willing to continue to feel torn, stupid and ashamed for not being true to herself. Living in constant anxiety and fear is not the life of the believer. She decided she could no longer cooperate with being berated, isolated, and imprisoned.

No matter how imperfect she was, she didn't deserve to be treated like this. As she woke up from the fog, she knew this was not Christ's desire for her faith walk. Self-recrimination was not the answer. She was not going to tell herself, "Well, at least he doesn't…." anymore.

She realized that the honest way of communicating assertively was good for her but did not change her husband. She could not heal Richard. She could not be forthright with him because he used it against her. She had to move into a silent strategizing, keeping peace as much as possible while trying to figure out what to do.

Identify Top Misgivings about Leaving

We can get on a treadmill of waiting on God and not doing what we can for ourselves. A mind weakened by abuse may fear taking the scary step out of bondage. Not acting in faith keeps us feeling less than. We will be challenged to please others instead of what we know we must do to live.

Our major challenge is to review all we have worked on so far. This reinforces what we know is true. We believed we could "save" or take responsibility away from our partners. Even God allows each person free will to choose their behaviors. We cannot change anyone. Abusers will continue to whisper in our ear that's it's our fault or scream at us to stay. We now know how to separate reality from their words.

A Word About Trauma Bonding

Trauma bonding is a common experience of those who have suffered the cycle of abuse. The pattern of intermittent reinforcement leaves the victim confused and demoralized. At this point, the victim feels loyalty to the abuser. They accept responsibility for the abuser's behavior toward them. This doubt about what is going on or your part in it is something you will have to resist. Know that you are not to blame. When you have misgivings, recognize them as a symptom of trauma bonding, another damaging effect of the abuse.

Perhaps the hardest pressure to deal with is emotional. We know we will deal with others who will not support us. Friends and sometimes family members are concerned but don't act. Church members may believe they should not encourage us to leave. Hymns, books, social media – all can contain messages to "stand by your man" or rely on God to do what we have already been given the power to do.

Our own fears for our children enter in. But they will thrive in an abuse -free home. It may be disruptive at first, but continuing to expose them to a home where we are abused is itself a danger for them.

'Life remains the same until the pain of remaining the same becomes . greater than the pain of change.

None of us want to say we have "failed". We have put everything we had into this relationship and it still hasn't worked. Our pride is certainly hurt. Many will tell us again that it was our responsibility to make it work. Again, they do not understand.

Every woman must get clear about these pressures.

Major **challenges** can be
- normal resistance to change
- conflicting emotions, part of trauma bonding
- our learned helplessness
- believing love can conquer all
- reluctance to give up hope
- emotional investment
- holding onto illusions
- fear of being alone.

Major **outer pressures** can be
- lack of support
- concerns about finances
- not knowing options
- legal considerations
- our reputation as Christian wives
- safety
- commitment to children.

Our lives, and perhaps our children's lives, are at stake. Overcoming these challenges is worth it. We must climb the walls of threats, fear, silence and confusion through our more mature faith in God.

We have now sorted out the confusion about faith concepts. Those who have not worked these through do not understand. We have gotten clear on why we are not to blame and why we cannot help him by staying. We will have to hold fast to this clarity. If we do, we will not return to the abuse.

Great!

The Spiritually Healthy Relationship

Respect

- respects individual values, beliefs, and ideas. (Matt 7:1-2)
- respects individual boundaries. (I Cor 15:23)
- encourages the growth of the core spiritual self with encouragement and praise (I Thess 5:11)

Honor

- encourages honest expression of spiritual growth and issues.(Prov 21:3)
- acknowledges feelings as real and valid. (Matt 9:36)
- allows each person to take responsibility without threats or condemnation.(Rom 8:1) •

Cherish

- seeks the wellbeing of the partner with empathy, patience and compassion. (II Cor 1:3-4)
- treats gently and tenderly as a valuable person(I Thess 2)

Comfort

- shares decision-making and daily responsibilities.(Gal 6:2)
- nurtures physical well-being, safety, comfort and assurance. (Ps 17:8)

Lovethispic.com

Recognize Invalid Pressures

The Abuser

Margary had locked herself in the bedroom to escape Richard, who was assaulting her. He broke down the door and raped her. When charged with marital rape, he unsuccessfully claimed that marriage was sacred and he had been under the influence of the devil.

Using the old excuse of the devil allows the abuser to escape responsibility for his behavior, which is calculated, conscious and deliberate. If called out in the church, he may make a show of repenting. Then the woman is accused of being hard hearted if she does not accept his repentance. But most have found these are false promises, again done to manipulate how others see him.

As in the actual abuse, the same tactics intensify to keep you from leaving. Even though abusers may have a steady stream of victims, they don't want to "lose" a victim. Attempts at Fear and Shame for Power and Control will increase. There are no limits that an abuser will use to justify abusing you.

If he senses you are considering leaving or not accepting abuse anymore, he may switch to the honeymoon stage. He may promise you to do what you ask him to, such as go to counseling, repent, promise to change, and other ploys. However for most abusers, this is part of the game. To test it, stay away for six months. If he wants to change, he will. Few can hold the pretense of changing for that long.

He may play upon your good nature and your desire to be supportive. He may suggest you are being hardhearted, or unforgiving, or unwilling to try again. These delaying tactics are tempting. Recognize them as part of trauma bonding.

If you relent, it weakens your position the next time you have had enough. He will believe you less. Honoring yourself will be harder. You now know you cannot keep cutting yourself up in little pieces to be in the relationship. But if you have left and returned, do not give up.

Misused Bible References

Richard hurled Bible verses at Margary, saying she was displeasing God. He considered himself above scrutiny, not subject to its teachings himself. He used the Word as a double-edged sword to keep her under his control. You have experienced this too.

Abusers use Bible verses selectively. Only verses that seem to support his agenda are used. Other views are not allowed. Bible verses should be viewed through the lens of God as love, Jesus' revelation. He chided hypocritical religious leaders who used the sacred texts to oppress and reject people in need.

Rom 5:3-5 is a favorite misused verse to keep us from protesting being mistreated. "We rejoice in our sufferings, because we know suffering produces perseverance, character, hope. And hope does not put us to shame, because God's love has been poured into our hearts through the Holy Spirit who has been given to us."

This is a misuse of this verse. This was written to Christians being persecuted for being Christians. Your husband is not supposed to be the one persecuting you. Being Godlike is being loving.

The legalistic use of the Bible leads to death, just as Jesus said. "It is the Spirit that quickens" (John 6:63 KJV). Using Jesus' words to keep women in bondage is not a legitimate use of Scripture. Jesus teachings are not to be used to hurt but to heal.

Misled Counselors or Church Leaders

When Margary sought help, they encouraged her to look toward her reward in heaven or to rely on God to bring good out of the situation. Leaving was not allowed. Either they did not confront Richard or they did not hold him accountable. "Christian" counselors merely repeated the same views. The burden was always on Margary.

It is important where you seek counsel. If a church emphasizes measuring up in the eyes of members, fear of revealing faults, or even threats of shunning to control behavior, the abuser often uses those practices to hide or inflict more pressure on his victim. Are they more concerned about the reputation of the church than your well-being? Are the women who urge you to stay afraid you will show more courage than they have? What is behind the tremendous pressure to keep a woman in pain but not to hold the husband accountable? It does not seem to be a genuine concern for her spiritual health.

Staying in the marriage outweighs the sanity, safety and health of the wife and children. They see leaving as more sinful than abuse. Some seem more concerned about the church's image than you. Other women may fear that their husbands or pastors may berate them for not making you stay. The pressure to maintain an image that all is well is heavy, but you do not worship the god of social approval.

Some genuinely care about you, but their comments are not helpful. Be aware that often they are not coming from the same experiences or frame of reference as you. You can assure them you appreciate their efforts, but you are not asking for their permission or approval to pursue your own well-being. Be aware they are coming from what might be true for them, but you are not asking them to take the same steps as you are. You will meet many who have walked your path and do understand. When you do, you will be amazed at the similarities in your stories.

> ### *Why Do Some Caring Christians Keep Feeling Guilty?*
>
> Have you noticed that some good people do all they can to help others but still feel guilty? Meanwhile people who hurt others don't seem to be bothered at all.
>
> It may have begun when they were young. Children tend to blame themselves for how they are treated.
>
> If adults cannot take care of them emotionally or physically, children develop feelings of shame, guilt, worthlessness, fear or hopelessness. Some children keep trying harder and harder to please. Other children may give up on ever being cared for.
>
> As adults, the children who keep trying constantly criticize themselves unfairly. These beliefs need therapy for healing, both emotionally and mentally. Even though they believe God loves them, they have trouble feeling it.
>
> It is hard to face this inner pain. Even worse, sometimes a powerful person may tell them to just follow him and he will make everything ok. Sometimes he will pretend to care about them just to use them.
>
> Then, they continue to feel bad about themselves. Even though this is painful, it is at least familiar. But the powerful person who is misusing them does not feel guilty. They tell the hurting person it is their fault if they still hurt. The guilt of never feeling loved becomes an emotional treadmill.

Uninformed Faith Media

Some books with encouraging titles do not support you in trying to decide. These books, articles or electronic productions can still apply a one-teaching-fits-all approach that upholds male privilege.

Isn't that kind of what this book is doing?

In *Competent to Counsel*, a Christian counseling training book, the author Jay Adams states that only adultery and desertion are grounds for divorce. There is no discussion in the book of abuse, trauma*, or other conditions of emotional, mental, physical or spiritual

threat. Self-defense is not allowed. Apparantly trying to break down a partner's soul is not considered desertion. In reality, abuse qualifies as desertion under the legal definition.

The Relationship Principles of Jesus by a minister at a large Southern Baptist church in California disallows abused women from leaving their marriage. The relationship is paramount. If the wife cannot leave, the husband is not held to equal responsibility.

On the other hand, a woman may better understand what this means. Joyce Myer wrote that a women's decision to divorce is between her and her God. In *The Battlefield for Your Mind*, (1995 Warner Books). she writes that justifying any behavior that God condemns is a dangerous thing (p. 79) and that "God does not want us to live under the tyranny of unjust expectations."(p.83). Each woman must clarify for herself her own path. It is her life that is on the line.

There is a difference between rational relying on God and accepting abuse. Meyer gives an example in the chapter on "Joy" about Kent Crockett who was upset. His wife had paid $7 more for gas at the full- service pump than the self -service one. Then he realized, she writes, that he had sold his joy for $7. He was willing to look at himself and apologized.

Your situation as an abused wife would have changed the story. In your situation, your husband would begin railing at you with Bible verses about being a fool. Or worse. Wouldn't a loving husband be glad his wife had assistance and not consistently find fault?

Electronic media is multiplying from different Christian organizations, each one adding a voice about why women must submit. It can seem as if no one understands. But more faith communities are understanding and are ready to help the woman of faith needing support.

*The index shows "trauma" on p 6 but I could not find any reference or discussion of it on that page.

Unaware Community

Margary was reluctant to seek help from any community agencies. This was shamed as "airing dirty laundry" or encouraging people in "the world" to have negative views of believers. Some members in the community did not want to get involved in faith matters or did not understand how her faith struggles influenced her unwillingness to leave.

Finally, however, since her church would not help her, she had to seek help in desperation. She found that her fears were greatly exaggerated and that there were indeed people who would help her without asking her to abandon her beliefs. Not recognizing how faith systems may enforce battering, community members are surprised to learn the extent of Biblical battering. They may feel both marriage and faith are private affairs. However, civil laws are being broken. Church members and leaders have been exposed as abusers. Jesus' teaching to help our neighbors is clear.

When we receive the Holy Spirit as a believer, we experience the fruits of the Spirit, which is not torment. Ignore those who encourage you to stay with a partner who abuses you in the name of God. His behavior damages your faith walk. Some may be more concerned about an image in the church, rather than what God says, your safety and your spiritual well-being. Your victimhood is not redemptive witness.

Your Bottom Line

Now that you are clear on the how your faith has been misused, you can make decisions with a clearer head and heart about staying. You know that staying will not change him. You know that staying will continue the current abuse you are experiencing.

You know you have given him more chances that he deserved. He has no interest in a healthy partnership. Most importantly, you now know that it is not God's will for you to live like this.

You want to return to nurturing your relationship with God. To commune in peace and hear God's voice, you cannot be constantly fighting for your life. Commit to God anyone who uses scripture to justify evil-doing.

You do have a choice. You realize that you do have the power to stop the abuse. Every accusation should be applied to your abuser. Every command to you should be exacted of the abuser. You begin to make new choices, new decisions, and exercise new skills. We can change our minds about what we are willing to accept, change how we react, and regain health in body, mind, heart and soul.

Increasingly more people are recognizing the misuse of God and the Bible in domestic violence. That means there are going to be more people who will support you. But remaining exposed to it daily will not help you regain peace with God and heal from its effects.

Claim Your Rewards for Releasing Him to God

You now realize that, for whatever reason, you have been misled into taking responsibility for your partner's free will, which even God cannot do. You should now feel freer to focus on your own health and wellbeing. Healing from this extensive trauma is God's will.

Recovery is no small task. It will take all your energy to heal emotionally, mentally and physically. Spiritually, you can now stop the torment. Claim your inheritance as God's beloved. Live in freedom and peace as you were meant to. Your body stores truth. It can recover when you resume self-care.

 Dignity You will return to being in touch with your real self, the loving woman who has so much good to offer the world. You will capture again that inner glow in your heart that comes from being in touch with the Holy Spirit of peace, joy and wisdom.

 Respect You will become stronger in honoring yourself. No longer giving your essence away, you will hold your head up, knowing you deserve respect as a woman of God.

92

**True Purpose** You will be able to follow freely what is yours to do. You know that being fully developed is God's will for you. You are unique. Honoring yourself, discovering your expression and sharing it, you will resume your path of spiritual healing and growth.

Letter to Those Who Do Not Understand:

———————————————————————————

———————————————————————————

———————————————————————————

My Prayer: "Dear God, my journey has taken me through to a deeper and broader understanding of your will. I realize now that I didn't want to admit I couldn't make this work. I was trying to do something that was against your will. A relationship takes two people. I thought You and me could do it, but that is not true. My partner is not willing to respect me as his partner.

I again need courage to take the necessary steps to live in the freedom of my faith. I know you are with me. I know you desire health, happiness, and peace for me and all your people. I need to keep my eyes focused on you as my source, not other's opinions. I am trusting that you will lead me to those who support me, who understand your greatness and love. Thank you. Amen."

"There comes this turning point-this clarifying moment in time-when you realize wide-eyed and terrified-your bondage is going to destroy you and permanently scar those you love. Thank God for it. It's a gift. A plane flying through the sky trailing this banner: TIME TO BREAK FREE." Beth Moore

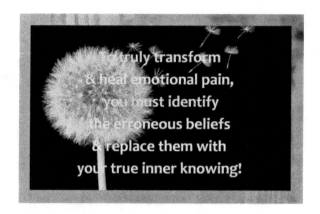

To truly transform & heal emotional pain, you must identify the erroneous beliefs & replace them with your true inner knowing!

*The exercise pages are great— super helpful for personal reflection

CHAPTER 7: EXERCISE

Claim your rewards for releasing him to God

You began this relationship wanting to follow God. You still do. The good we say or do is living expression of Christ within us. The elements of Jesus ministry are love/compassion, faith, wisdom/truth, and integrity. To be a clear channel for God, we have to establish a place of peace within. Your rewards for insisting on that place by releasing him include four conditions:

1. Freedom from guilt and shame- these states are not part of the life of a believer
2. Dignity – as someone who has known the love of God, you have dignity
3. Respect – God has respected the divine creation that you are; as such others must as well
4. True Purpose- to be an example of the abundant life God desires for us all through abiding in God

1.   What was your identity before your abuse? How can you begin to reclaim some of that? Are there pictures? School records? Past friends? Activities you liked?

2.   What are the most difficult parts of the abuse to talk about? What was the key way you lost dignity? Respect? Freedom? and purpose?_____

_____

3.   What are some of the beliefs you had about happy marriage that you had? List the ways you are not to blame. Rather than labeling this a "failure", how can you define this experience?_____

_____

4.   What are some resources you have found that are strengthening your mind, heart, and spirit?

_____

_____

5.   More people are becoming aware of how subtle and pervasive the pressures are to keep women in abusive relationships, even in churches. Have you found any other women or information that reflects your experience? _____

_____

6.   Now that you know you have done all you can and that no one can change their abusive partner except God, how will you begin to release these unreasonable expectations of yourself?_____

_____

Here are some non-committal or neutral statements that provide space for you to avoid compromising yourself when challenged:

"I hadn't thought of that."

"That's an interesting way to look at it."

"I see things differently."

Ask about more information on topics without correcting. Just listen.

Sometimes a simple "Oh" is enough of a response.

Remember there are people who are not well but beyond your power to help.

Detach* to maintain your peace. You know you cannot change him. You have tried to get him help many times and he has refused. You know there is not a good reason for you or your family to be destroyed. Focus on moving ahead with what you know is true for you and avoid engaging in conflict. Let go and let God.

*Millions have healed themselves of resentment with this AA prayer. While you do not need to live with people who hurt you, you can help heal your heart by praying this prayer, taken from p. 552 of AA's *The Big Book* (2005). Many have to pray it a lot longer, and it is not to be a source of guilt if you are not free right away. But you do this for your own health, not to excuse how they harmed you.

"If you have a resentment you want to be free of, if you will pray for the person or the thing that you resent, you will be free. If you will ask in prayer for everything you want for yourself to be given to them, you will be free. Ask for their health, their prosperity, their happiness, and you will be free. Even when you don't really want it for them, and your prayers are only words and you don't mean it, go ahead and do it anyway. Do it every day for two weeks and you will find you have come to mean it and to want it for them, and you will realize that where you used to feel bitterness and resentment and hatred, you now feel compassionate understanding and love."

CHAPTER 8: DELIVERANCE

MARGARY'S
STORY

Now I realized my deliverance was an inside job.

I saw that no matter what I did, he was choosing to mistreat me. My support did not come from any single faith community.

I called a prayer service for help. Even though I would call at different times, I would talk with the same sweet woman. I later learned this was not usual. To me it was God's angel helping me through this unknown woman. Her consistent, loving support helped me through nights of fear.

I wrote to a leading televangelist's wife and received a personal letter, not the typical form letter of support. She did not tell me to ignore, accept, or make excuses for my husband. She did not tell me to stay to save him. She did not tell me to submit or obey. A wise woman of faith knows the difference between using the Bible for support or as a club.

A group of women from another church encircled me in prayer, Their belief was to rebuke the evil I was under. They did not tell me to "suffer for Christ's sake" or "offer it up to God" or "wait patiently". They knew he was not going to listen to Scripture when it said to be slow to anger and to rule his spirit (Prov. 16:32). They understood Richard was not living as a believer. They understood we were not accomplishing any work for the kingdom of God.

All of these women helped me grow stronger and stand taller for me and my children. When I reached out to men ministers or "Christian" counselors, only one suggested I should not go home with Richard if I felt afraid.

The next to the last time I left, I found a small one- bedroom apartment in one of three old brick buildings built around a courtyard. It was on the bus line so I could get to work and the kids to school. A stray bunny gave the kids something fun to focus on. For one night and a moment, we felt free. But he lured me back with promises to go to counseling. All he really wanted was my three paychecks I would get at the end of the school year. He cleaned out my bank account after they were deposited.

I realized there would never be a good time to leave. I was not going to let him drive us out unprepared again, because that meant I always ended up going back. Money or no money, I would have to make Plan A, Plan B and Plan Z.

After he left for a meeting the next morning. I had a few clothes in a suitcase and we drove to Kansas City. I had arranged to stay temporarily at a friend's. I had alerted her that he would take the car to keep me from going to work, trying to keep me dependent. He followed us and did take the car during the third night.

I would have to cut any ties he had to me or he would continue to harass us.

Good

QUESTIONS

1. *What were my skills before I got involved with him?*
2. *What do others compliment me on?*
3. *What did I enjoy doing before I married?*
4. *What are some of my dreams?*
5. *What creates the greatest pressure for me right now?*
6. *Who can I trust to understand and support me?*
7. *What resources are free to help me get through each day?*

Margary began using her spiritual power for her own well- being, not to cooperate with someone hurting her in God's name. Putting her oxygen mask on first meant honoring her own intuition, listening to God's voice of love within her – these were skills that obeyed and honored God's will for her. She had a lot to learn and a lot to unlearn.

She had to be patient and gentle with herself as she made her way back to her God-given dignity. Wallowing in condemning herself because she had submitted to abuse would not help her move forward.

The first breakthrough was admitting that it's normal to be angry when being hurt. So many believers quoted "Be ye angry and sin not," and to them sinning meant not obeying. They placed the burden on her, not Richard. She knew God had not abandoned her, and to remain close to God she could not continue to cooperate with abuse. That would be spiritual and perhaps physical death.

You now realize God wants you to honor yourself because God does. "Love forever; hate never" is an impossible myth. We will have losses in life and we will have to grieve them. Some of the hardest losses are illusions. To "let go" does not mean to stop caring. It means you can't do it for someone else. We have taken too much responsibility and not trusted God to take care of what we cannot. Just for today respect your boundaries and act as a child of God, destined to live in freedom, peace and safety, deserving of love. Forgive yourself for tolerating the invalidation and pain you received from someone you thought cared about you. He lied.

LEVEL 6 OBJECTIVES– You Know You Shouldn't Stay But You Don't Know How To Get Out

Faith Concept: Wisdom

In this chapter, you will…

> *Evaluate your strengths, challenges and resources*
> *Identify small and larger steps to take*
> *Plan your defense against the most common sabotaging tactics and*
> *   pressures*
> *Develop Plans A, B and Z*
> *Take One Step, One Day at a Time*

Evaluate Your Strengths, Challenges and Resources

Your tremendous strengths have been disparaged. Now you need to focus them on your well-being. As a woman you are under heavy pressures to satisfy other's demands before your own needs. To do this involves self-betrayal, not being willing to be honest about our thoughts and feelings. This subjection breeds shame, alienation and disconnection from our bodies. So a good place to start is with our bodies. Relaxation, good nutrition, gentle exercise, and other aids are ways to honor our bodies as the gifts from God they are. Mental and emotional therapy is not a luxury but necessities for us. Journaling, meditation, counseling, and other ways to reclaim and express ourselves are essential to our healing. Creativity and beauty, whether in nature, music, art, or other forms, are important ways to restore our souls.

Check your assets you have or need to regain:
Spiritual:
_____ my faith that God loves me
_____ truth that sustains me
_____ a good heart
_____ true friends

_____ other_____

Emotional:
_____determination
_____courage
_____persistence
_____empathy
_____other_____

Mental:
_____discernment
_____wisdom
_____ability to reason
_____education
_____other_____

When you come out of abuse, you realize you've been living somebody else's dream.

- Lynn Andrews

Physical:
_____strength
_____finances
_____home
_____transportation
_____other_____

Identify Small and Larger Steps

If you are working on this level, you have already done many of the "next indicated, right things" that you can. Perhaps most importantly is to have access to a support group who are not afraid to stand with you against your abuser.

Undermining your financial resources is a strong ploy. Every small victory that means you can stay free will encourage you. So plan your access to money or other resources before you cut ties. Margary was a target for a financial scam from a woman posing as her friend. Avoid giving money away or becoming financially responsible for someone who says they want to help you at this time. Rental and utility agreements can leave you with bills you did not create if you make them with suddenly "new" friends.

Although police have seen abusers before, you may have been told that no one would believe you. A favorite threat is that you won't be able to make it without him. Of course the reality or truth is that you will be better off than ever without the abuse. No matter how bad it got after Margary left, it was still better than living with the abuse. It is highly difficult, especially in a small community, to stay in the same area as the abuser. The general rule with those who have this personality disorder is no contact. That is because they interpret contact as an opening to continue control and manipulation.

There is an advantage if there can be some geographic distance between you and the abuser if possible. If not, do not let that prevent you from escaping. Just plan for the pressures that you know he and perhaps others will bring.

Although many abusers don't want to risk going to jail, be aware that the possibility of a death threat will be carried out and have your security measures in place.

Abusers at first may feel they have nothing to lose if you are leaving and seek the ultimate solution to not having you as an available victim.

Margary was fortunate that her husband did not want to lose his freedom and so, as many bullies, his threats of killing her were bluffs. Also the manipulative nature of abusers often means that they will switch to charming around a third party. That means you want to have a third party, a witness, around interactions with him, even if it is only a public place.

Avoid any romantic entanglements, however, because predators see a woman in distress and realize she is vulnerable. Abusers are persistent for a while until they go on to their next victim. Even though Margary changed her phone number for 30 days, Richard was there waiting for to begin harassing her on the phone after the 30 days was up. Just continue to not buy into the pressures and abusers will move on. They operate on payoffs for them and when they stop getting them, they move on.

Anticipate Sabotaging Tactics and Pressures

Promises, crying, increased threats and guilt trips will be used to try to break you down even further. You have learned many ways to neutralize these tactics. Continue to chart, relabel, journal and use assertive communication. By now most of the ploys are no surprise.

Here is where the lack of community support, especially from your faith community, may be the hardest for you. It is one thing to have the courage to stop sacrificing your life for his arrogant needs. It is another to have the organization and people whom you have supported and befriended try to shame you into staying against your wellbeing. They may even feel they are doing the right thing but you know it is not the case. As we have realized, the church that urges you to stay in a dishonoring relationship - or rejects you if you leave - clearly is not following Jesus' example of compassion and support for the oppressed. It is the religious equivalence of the old civil laws that considered domestic battering not an assault.

Margary's social status as a minister's wife added extra pressures. However other women have been married to socially prominent abusers. Wives of policemen, doctors, lawyers and even judges have taken the extra planning steps necessary to escape. It can be done. You just have to plan for pressures related to their position that may be at work. Their social position does not mean they are immune from this personality disorder.

You will find others who understand and who will support you. In fact, you might be amazed at the number of women of faith or prominent men's wives who have left because it is not talked about. But you are not alone. Your life is more valuable than saving face or social status. Living your faith freely is the life God wants for you. Others may be threatened by your bravery. Whatever the reason for their not supporting you, it is not because they understand. They are not with you in the home facing these attacks.

Do not give up on yourself. You will break free. Do not accept the common accusations you may hear:

- You are weak. You can't make it on your own.
- If you try to leave once and don't make it, you will never be able to get out.

- You should stay if you still love him.
- You should not leave if there is no physical violence. ✓
- Your emotional turmoil is a sign you should stay.
- If the abuser promises to change for the 1,000th time, you must take him back.
- You will continue to make the same mistakes even if you leave.
- You can't have a healthy relationship in the future because you are damaged.
- It will be easy to heal and get on with your life.
- Everyone who wants to help you has your best interest at heart.
- If you have second thoughts, it means you should stay.
- You can have the same relationship with him as before he abused you.
- Can't you give him another chance?
- What about the children?
- You need to pray and believe.
- You will go to hell if you break your vow.
- Are you sure you know what you are doing?
- He seemed like such a good man. ✓
- Whatever will you do?
- You'll never make it without him.
- No one else will want you.

or any of the other words that invalidate what you know and experience.

You are not betraying your faith.
You are not betraying Jesus' teachings.
You are not obeying God's will by suffering abuse.
The abuse damages your faith and your relationship with God.
The fruits of the Spirit are not present.
You are not responsible for your husband's behavior.
You are not responsible for healing him (saving him through faith, love, prayer, forgiveness, etc.)
If you believe in a forgiving God, set your pride aside, admit the relationship is not working, and ask for forgiveness for leaving if that will help you allow yourself to get out.

Develop Plans A, B and Z

Women who are already weakened in body, mind, heart and soul are to be applauded and supported for going even further to establish a life of wholeness. Most of us feel like we just need to go to a retreat center for a month or longer, but our responsibilities continue while we are recovering. By refusing to leave until we can stay gone, we give ourselves a better chance to use our energy well. The processing in this workbook helps build an inner foundation of assurance. This helps you withstand pressures to return. However if you have to make several attempts to get out, do not despair.

Perhaps the most difficult aspect for a woman of faith to accept is that, because you are dealing with a deceptive individual who is shrewd, you may have to mislead him in order to escape. Ask for forgiveness if you must. Small evasions or misdirections merely level the playing field if being honest with him is used against you. Consider a war victim trying to escape. If you could misdirect your guard to get out, you would do it. This is no less a war situation since you have been made a prisoner of war in your mind, heart and soul.

Actions under coercion are not part of our true selves. Of course, if we can avoid this, we do. But if we can't, we don't beat ourselves up further over it. Jesus often used a "need to know" approach and even refused to give details that could be used against him. For example, He would use questions to answer insincere approaches. He even told a man not to tell anyone he had been healed. He knew the consequences would be untimely and adverse at that point in His plan.

Plan A is the first one, made up of the small steps you can take in your current situation. You now objectively can predict his behavior. Richard had a history of robbing her of all of earnings and had even fraudulently cleaned out her separate bank account. Margary gradually established a secret fund she could access that he could not. After she fled, he even got a policeman to track her down by feigning concern for her disappearance. When the policeman found her, he sensed that she had left because she was afraid. He then realized this was a domestic abuse situation and told Richard he couldn't find her.

Richard then tried to break into the next place Margary had moved to. When she heard him rattling the door knob, she called 911. When police arrived, he told them she had asked him to change the locks for her. Of course they were not deceived and removed him.

So Plan B went into effect. Margary went to the second safe house that she had arranged. By that time the authorities had a record that she was hiding from an abusive husband and did not pursue her, Since Margary was known in the community as the pastor's wife, she was reluctant to use the shelter where they were living because of professional relationships with the staff. Shelters also may be full or not in your area. But that does not mean you have no recourse.

My point is that you do not plan only on one level. You know your abuser. You know his tactics. Plan for them and then go at least two levels beyond that.

"Be ye wise as serpents and harmless as doves." Jesus instructed followers to do this as they went out to interact with others about God. Surely it no less applies to you who are seeking to live in freedom from a persecutor. List some concerns you have as you begin to plan.

Letter to Those Who Would Sabotage Me:

_____

_____

_____

My Prayer: "Dear God, you have led me all through my life. You know my heart. Thank you for helping me learn more light. Now I must act on my faith. You are there before me, behind me and all around me and within me. You are in those who would help me. Stand with me as I use the wisdom you give me to meet any obstacles to my freedom. Thank you. Amen."

What really scares the narcissist is your ability to succeed without them and in spite of their attempts to destroy you. Shahida Arabi

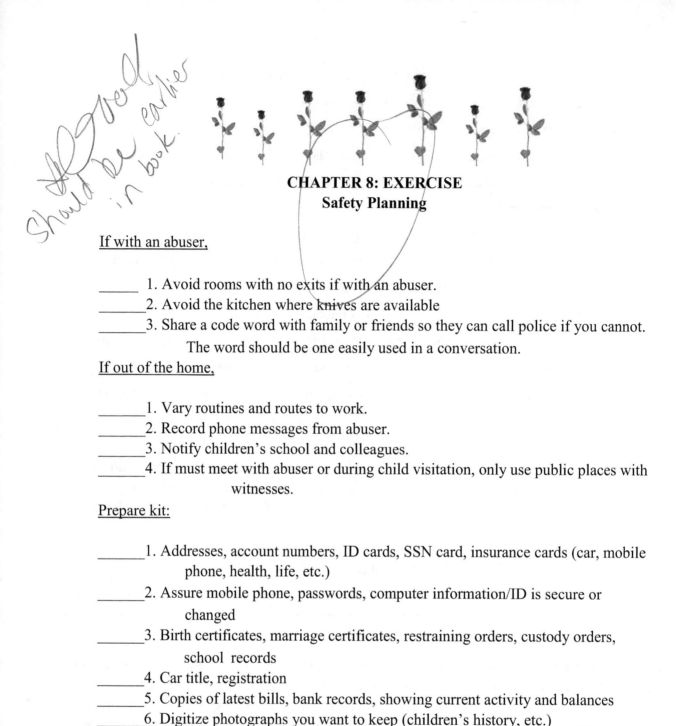

Should be earlier in book [handwritten note]

CHAPTER 8: EXERCISE
Safety Planning

<u>If with an abuser,</u>

_____ 1. Avoid rooms with no exits if with an abuser.

_____ 2. Avoid the kitchen where knives are available

_____ 3. Share a code word with family or friends so they can call police if you cannot. The word should be one easily used in a conversation.

<u>If out of the home,</u>

_____ 1. Vary routines and routes to work.

_____ 2. Record phone messages from abuser.

_____ 3. Notify children's school and colleagues.

_____ 4. If must meet with abuser or during child visitation, only use public places with witnesses.

<u>Prepare kit:</u>

_____ 1. Addresses, account numbers, ID cards, SSN card, insurance cards (car, mobile phone, health, life, etc.)

_____ 2. Assure mobile phone, passwords, computer information/ID is secure or changed

_____ 3. Birth certificates, marriage certificates, restraining orders, custody orders, school records

_____ 4. Car title, registration

_____ 5. Copies of latest bills, bank records, showing current activity and balances

_____ 6. Digitize photographs you want to keep (children's history, etc.)

Check which items in Safety Planning you need to secure.

Write about other concerns or plans you need to make. List those who may help you.

_____

_____

_____

A Word About Social Media

Limit or close your social media accounts. With cameras everywhere, abusers have been known to entrap victims with staged videotapes. Listen to warning signs within. If your abuser invites you to a meeting with him and then tries to get you upset, he may be collecting video of you acting irrationally. He can use these against you on social media or even in a courtroom. Remember manipulators are masters of image. Also be selective in your news feed or friends.

Community Forces

Misperceptions, stigma, or stereotypes may mean some community support you expected will fall through. Be able to recognize and plan for ways around or through these by accessing those who understand the battering syndrome, how faith is misused, or gender stereotypes may work against your wellbeing. Continue to meet with support groups.

1. Sense of disbelief
2. Shunning or blaming you
3. Lack of action
4. Neutral stance or silence
5. Misguided counseling
6. Enabling the abuser
7. Misinformation
8. Bureaucratic delays

Which ones have you already encountered?_____

Which ones will you need to prepare to meet?_____

List resources you still need to secure:

My Plan A:

A, safety_____

B. resources (money, food, shelter, transportation, child care, school, etc.)

C. people_____

My Plan B:_ A.Safety_____

 B. Resources (money food, shelter, transportation, child care, school, etc.

C. people_____

My Plan C:

A.   safety_____

B. resources (money, food, shelter, transportation, child care, school, etc.)

 C. people_____ and

on....

Stay with what works, what keeps you in God's peace. Honor yourself by choosing to feel, think. You have a right to exist, to have needs respected. Surrender the inner critic to God to heal.

CHAPTER 9: DEVELOPMENT

MARGARY'S

STORY

I found that there are people who have love in their hearts, and they are not always in the church.

Three women - a neighbor, a supervisor and a friend -had helped me escape with a few clothes but no furniture. I would start a new job in August but this was May. I took a sub-minimum wage job to survive until August.

When food stamp workers told me I didn't qualify, I got food donations from charities. He harassed me at work and showed up at the house. Once he tried to break in. He told the police I had asked him to change the locks but they knew better.

My new job was 20 miles away. I woke up and found the car gone. I knew he would do this to try to get me fired. My neighbor had agreed to let me use her car if he did. I would take her to her job, go to mine, and pick her back up after work. I alerted my supervisor about what he might try to do. She agreed to keep him off my job site. Even with these arrangements in place, he came to my job and screamed obscenities. He dumped our clothes on the lawn before security came. I took precautions.

I picked the kids up from school and stayed at a motel that night. He did not return in the next few days. He valued his freedom. An abuser will always do what is in his best interest. My friends alerted me that he returned to Wichita but he harassed by phone. I changed the number for 30 days but he was there screaming when the number changed back. I finally didn't answer the phone because I didn't want to hear his foul words.

In the divorce, I got the house, the debt and custody. He got visitation rights which he never used. This was a blessing because it meant less upset for the kids. He had only used them to get to me. I sold the house at a loss and moved with no forwarding address. At times, I didn't know how we were going to make it financially. We had pressed board furniture and ate spaghetti with Velveeta. But it was still better than the torment we had been living in.

As the years went by, finances improved and we had peace. We could sleep in safety. We went to counseling. While I can't say that my children completely healed, there was space to work on it. I found a group of believers who supported me after my church turned its back on me.

I learned to speak my voice again. In that first year, I talked almost nonstop to anyone about anything because I had been forbidden to talk for so long. The skills I had learned to escape helped me in my job. I kept getting stronger.

Do you believe God is with you?

QUESTIONS:

1.   *What do you need to do first?*
2.   *Who or what is in your support system?*
3.   *Who or what can you add to that system?*
4.   *What self-care is most challenging for you?*
5.   *What self-criticisms do you need to release?*

LEVEL 7 OBJECTIVES– You Get Out but You Need to Recover

Faith Concept: Wholeness (Holiness)

In this chapter, you will…

> *Assess the damage*
> *Manage daily pressures and support*
> *Identify your most pressing healing needs*
> *Identify three ways to regain your experience as God's beloved*

All the threats were false. He used to tell Margary she would never make it without him, that no one would ever want her. No man did seem to want her… to be free. Her brother- in- law said to put her children up for adoption. Only one pastor did not advocate her husband's oppression, no matter how much she was suffering. Most felt loyal to other men, even if she and her children were in danger. Most disappointing, many church women seemed afraid to not go along with them. It took a long time for Margary to find a supportive faith community.

God is love and love is the chief doctrine Jesus taught. Margary had misinterpreted what that meant or rather she had believed how it was misused. She had loved and not received love in return. That was not what the Great Commandment meant.

The manipulative games are what they trust. Just stop believing them. Because the truth is the opposite. Margary did better than she ever had. What happened to her had happened to other women. She found people who appreciated her. She found ways to use her talents. Her heart was free to love and relate to Christ within, in freedom.

She found life once she stopped believing that God wanted death.

Assess the Damage

You are not to blame because you need healing.
You have not been wounded because you are defective, need to be punished, or evil.

The most common damages for those of us who experienced this level of abuse are

- flashbacks
- anxiety
- demoralization
- depression
- doubting self-worth
- hypervigilance
- overcoming residual guilt and shame
- racing thoughts,
- regret over lost opportunities
- sleeping and eating disturbances
- sorrow at loss of self
- pressures from others and from within to return

It is at this point that we do not need platitudes: someone telling us we just have a lack of faith, need to repent, or that if we go back these will go away. This is retraumatization.

Women of faith can cringe at memories of betraying themselves under attack. CPSTD is Complex Post-Traumatic Stress Syndrome – it features the normal symptoms of Post-Traumatic Stress but adds another level. This trauma is prolonged and repetitive in a relationship of unequal power. Some believers mistakenly enforced this uneven power. They only looked at part of God's total word.

CPTSD arises when entrapment is a factor, a viable escape route is not available. If you are not free to move about or leave, you are in an entrapment situation. Legally it is known as forcible detainment. It's just that the chains are in our minds, hearts and spirits even if the physical restraints are not in place.

Helplessness and losing our sense of self and identify mark CPTSD. We feel fundamentally broken. We doubt our competency, even though we are over-responsible.

Women who hold full time jobs, take care of five children, volunteer at their church, and keep house will apologize for not measuring up. This makes recovery harder but it also points to the first order of business: the rebuilding of self and our sense of competency.

Judith Herman first described these effects in her 1992 book, Trauma and Recovery. Small steps involve identifying what we are afraid to do, even in something as small as learning to drive, and doing it. Art therapy is helpful here because many of us have had our creativity stomped out of us. To learn to speak our opinions again, to paint a flower pot, to take a walk in the woods, are all small ways we re-experience normal freedom and self-sufficiency. Be patient with your progress and find those who will acknowledge and validate your courage.

CPTSD Symptoms
▪ Emotional instability (mood swings)
▪ Forgetfulness
▪ Feeling essentially different from other human beings
▪ Perceiving the abuser as all powerful, even psychic or invincible
▪ Failure to protect self
▪ Despair
▪ Sorrow
▪ Depression
▪ Hypervigilance (an effect of not feeling safe)
▪ Feeling disloyal for displeasing others or for normal needs

Hypervigilance is living with an attitude of always being on your guard, always scanning your surroundings and being easily startled. Some women break down in tears if they accidentally bump their arm. With our reserves so depleted, any small request can be the straw that broke the camel's back.

You understand now you are struggling with the result of prolonged and repetitive abuse and not some essential flaw in yourself. The abuser is quick to ridicule you for the effects of his abuse, another way to avoid responsibility. Reject these interpretations. One writer who left religious abuse reported she was only partially healed even 3 years later. (Jacqui, Nov. 10, 2016, verbalabusejournals.com, Brainwashing section.) Certainly staying is not the answer.

> "People often don't realize there's a difference between generalized anxiety and anxiety associated with PTSD. For those of us with PTSD, it's not about what might happen. It's about what did happen.
> Telling a person with PTSD to "just let go because worry won't fix anything" or "most of the things you worry about will never really happen" can not only be confusing to us but it can also be damaging. Because the things that cause our anxiety already happened. For us, it's not so much about worrying. it's about remembering." Judith Herman

yes! Its about remembering!

Manage Daily Pressures and Support

Part of our difficulty is that, when we need help, we have to be careful how we get it. We doubt our judgement. After all, we believed so seriously and were still duped. Console yourself that you now have more information to make better decisions. You are wiser than you were. Still, there will be times, perhaps when you hear one of your old songs or another trigger, that you will mourn or have misgivings. At these times, review your experience. Review the work you did to save your life and your children's lives if you have them. You overcame what many have not.

In recovery programs, a wise recommendation is to avoid serious relationships for a year. At this fragile time, it is tempting to find someone to help us, and we need and deserve help, but we have to choose wisely. Watch how people treat others before getting too involved. Stay at the friendship level if you can.
Because of finances women sometimes want a roommate. Avoid sharing a space if you can. Margary learned about false friends. One woman would not pay her share

of rent and utilities. Another betrayed a confidence at work. Margary began to criticize herself for being so blind or trusting. But she stopped and realized this was the old pattern: she could choose better now. She is not stupid for being a loving, giving person. The other person is unworthy of her help. She knew this was part of the healing cycle and she learned from it.

You may need childcare beyond school hours. Some women had boyfriends who were not a good choice for their children. Be careful and listen to your instincts. If you feel uneasy about the other person, honor that. There are some men and women who want to take advantage of our trauma to manipulate us even further. If this happens, do not beat yourself up. Learn from it and make better choices the next time.

Daily pressures are earning a living, child care, a home, rest, nutrition, health, and emotional care. Resources are knowledgeable counselors, books, support groups, and education. A college course was a tremendous help to Margary while she was struggling. She learned about manipulation and how to stop it. A group of women prayed with her and for her on a regular basis. An enlightened pastor defended her to her husband so that he was on the alert that someone else knew there was a risk, and one of her coworkers often helped with childcare at no cost. Her neighbor provided transportation when she needed it. Her supervisor backed her, keeping her employed and protected at the office. Continue to educate yourself with encouraging words. Holy Spirit is with you.

There will be people to help you without asking for your soul or your bank account in return. You will find that your mind is trustworthy again, that you can understand details, make good judgements, and get the information you need.

Identify Your Most Pressing Wounds for Healing

The emotions, memories and physical pains after leaving are the same that you had to overcome while in bondage: anxiety, fear, loneliness, anger, loss and grief do not go away because you are now out of immediate danger. You just have space to work on them sanely and safely now. Since your entire system has been attacked, you will need to take your time and determine what your greatest pressure points are. For example, Margary kept dreaming of her husband chasing or threatening her. She woke up exhausted and couldn't go to work. This is a common experience. Accept that, whatever you are experiencing, is normal and can be healed in stages.

Unless you are a survivor of emotional abuse you have no idea what it means to fight daily battles in your head with a person you no longer have contact with.

Verbal, emotional and physical abuse has residual effects on the survivor. You don't just "Get over it" !

Journaling helped Margary stop the constant whirling in her mind. A Harbinger Press workbook for domestic violence victims makes a good point about guilt. We cannot judge ourselves for what we did not know. We were doing the best we could at the time.

Counseling from someone who understands CPTSD is vital. Interview potential counselors to see if they understand women's needs, religious abuse issues as well as domestic violence.

Major healing tasks are
- Addressing traumatic memories
- Revising inner critic messages
- Mourning loss of what you wanted and what might have been
- Establishing healthy social relationships with healthy boundaries
- Reestablishing a sense of safety
- Trusting abilities to process information
- Regaining balance in nutrition, sleep, environment, and energy
- Regaining positive emotional experiences (like enjoyment, appreciation of beauty)
- Gaining strength to find out what might still be

Of course, if you have children, you have the difficult task of taking care of their needs as well as recovering yourself. As an educator, Margary had children in class and children at home. It was overwhelming many days and sometimes she did not think she could go on. Her saving grace was the 20-mile drive between work and home. This small break helped her stress. Later she joined a gym to build stamina. But she did go on and you will too. We are strong. We learn to use our strengths for our own well- being as well as our children. They will have their own issues and needs for counseling and healing. Be kind, gentle and patient with yourself and them. Together you will create a happier family.

A Word About Custody

*only really speaks to male abusers!

Margary was fortunate that her children's father no longer tried to see them. If you have shared custody or enforced visitation, try to make it in public or with a supervisor. If the children are too upset, you can ask the orders be changed because it is not in the children's best interest. The court is not always your friend but stay with it until you succeed.

Some men today seek custody so they do not have to pay child support. Some women have even been ordered to pay support to the father. If this is the case, use the social service system to overturn the decision by documenting abuses of visitation or support. Stay trusting in the good that God has for you. Your emerging from abuse is one way you know God is with you. Trust this to gain more evidences as you meet other challenges. One woman lost custody because of the lies the abuser brought to court. As hard as this was, it gave her time to heal. Meanwhile she continued to bring evidence to the court until she got her children back.

Whatever happens, it will pass. At least now you have the freedom to make decisions in your own and children's best interests. It's not a perfect world, but living free of abuse makes it better.

Regain Your Experience as God's Beloved

Three major ways to restore your experience of God's beloved are meditation, self-care, and supportive relationships. Carve out some time each day, even if in little spurts, for quiet, breathing, and affirming words. There are many good audible resources you can listen to that will rebuild your sense of entitlement and experience of God's love. This is not the time to focus on self-improvement but rather healing. You need rain and nutrition to flower now.

Self-care will involve more rest, saying "no" to demands, finding simple pleasures again, and treating your body gently. There will be time for returning to service later after you have regained a normal balance to your daily life. You are a domestic war veteran. You don't need to run a marathon just yet. What you are able to do each day will have to be enough.

Supportive relationships are hard to overemphasize. Stay with those who understand or at least can empathize with what you have been through. You have given much; be willing to find and ask a proven person for help with daily tasks, take children for an hour, visit a movie, walk in nature, or take late night calls. If you find you need to not talk with some people for awhile, feel free to do so.

In these ways your heart will once again be able to bask in God's love.

What Did We Learn?

What did Margary and others gain by going through this? What do we hope you gain?

Religious oppression died; spiritual freedom was born.

The fantasy of who our husbands were died; the freedom to be ourselves and feel good about it in Christ was born.

The misunderstanding of what Christ wanted died; the reality of the deliberate misuse of our faith to keep us controlled was born.

We learned each person's faith is very personal; no one else has the right to dictate it to us.

We found that our relationship with God is our business. We are responsible for keeping a heart of love wherein God can dwell. We don't owe anyone who interferes with that.

We realized that Christ did not die so we could live in bondage. The record of Jesus is one of freeing people from bondage, healing, forgiveness and human compassion, especially for the downtrodden, the helpless, including women. He had no patience for those who would place heavy burdens on people in the name of God. He had no patience when the scriptural law was used to oppress and not help.

We realized that the Bible could be used to tell us to develop our souls by denying our legitimate needs or the Bible could be used to help us develop our souls by using our God-given mind, body and will.

We learned the difference in being selfish and self-care; between humiliation and humility; between submission and surrender.

We learned that there are some willing to use God to create death rather than life.

We learned to face our thoughts and feelings honestly. We stopped being people pleasers and codependents. We stopped being afraid. We learned to stay with those who supported us. We realized that there were pressures- some benevolent, some not - in society, religion, media, school and parental - to separate us from ourselves. We learned this was not Christ's desire for us. We began our relationship thinking we were pursuing a fulfilling life of service to God with a loving husband. We emerged with our own relationship with God intact and stronger. Never again would we worship the idol of a man, a book or an organization. We would live freely in Christ.

So our faith concepts changed:

Obedience stopped being servitude to men and became relationship with God.

Submission stopped being painful and became letting go and letting God.

Forgiveness stopped being blind and became healing for ourselves

Pain stopped being exalted as God's major will and became just a part of human life, not sought but borne in healthy ways, not as martyrs.

The life of Christ within created our equality in God.

And this is what we want for you.

My Prayer: "Dear God, thank you for helping me see what you meant by the kingdom of God in me and those I love. It will take some time for me to heal. I know you will lead me to those helpers and wisdom to heal. I will make amends to myself, forgiving myself for allowing myself to be misused in your name. I will work to clear my heart of the pain so that I do not allow resentment to poison me. I will minister to my body with quiet, breathing, nutrition and any other nurturing activity you show me. In this way, I will obey in a new way, a way that honors me as your creation. Thank you. Amen."

"I learned not to believe in suffering. It is a form of death, a poison, that kills emotions."
Susan Fromberg Schaeffer, concentration camp survivor
Quoted in "A Battered Wife Survives: Letters from a War Zone." By Andrea Dworkin

"What some call rebellion, others call survival." – Shirley Fessel

CHAPTER 9: EXERCISES

You will continue to need to use the tools you have learned in this workbook. Charting, journaling, labeling, redefining, uncovering assumptions, assertive communication and self-care will continue to be important as you build your healthier life.

You know that there are many places where pressures are brought to try to keep women from fully functioning. However history shows that we will not be held back. God is our Encourager, Wisdom, Strength and Advocate. You have already proven your strength by surviving sophisticated and sanctioned attacks on your core as a person. You are more equipped now than ever.

In the days, weeks, months and years ahead, and sometimes just one moment at a time, it is important to record your support and progress. You can then reinforce and affirm your strengths as you review how far you have come.

1. What are some of the most disturbing thoughts that still whirl in your head, threatening your peace of mind?_____

    _____

2. What aspect of your affairs do you need to find additional support?

    _____

    _____

3. What has improved? What gratitudes have increased?_____

    _____

4. What new little joys, freedoms or powers have you discovered lately? What gifts have you found coming your way?_____

5.   Which self-care actions are helping to restore you? Positive meditations, exercise, music, coffee with a friend, a new creative activity? _____

My heart goes with you as you begin your journey out of bondage and into the sunlight of God's love for you. Many have gone before you, will accompany you, and rejoice in your redemption from Biblical Battering. We welcome you to the company of women who know their equal worth in God.

BIBLIOGRAPHY

Note: Recently many religious organizations have addressed domestic violence in churches and Christian homes. Some of these, however, continue to uphold male privilege. Every attempt has been made to include here only those resources which support a woman's decision to freely live her faith.

Books

Anderson, Jocelyn. *Women Submit: Christians and Domestic Violence.* San Mateo: One Way Café' Press, 2007.

Booth, Leo. *Breaking the Chains: Understanding Religious Addiction and Abuse.* Atlanta: Emmaus House Press, 1989.

Cloud, Henry and John Townsend. *Boundaries: When to Say Yes, How to Say No to Take Control of Your Life.* Grand Rapids: Zondervan Publishing, 1995.

Durve, Anisha. *The Power to Break Free Workbook.* Cleveland: The Power to Break Free Foundation. 2012.

Elgin, Suzette Haden. *You Can't Say That to Me: Stopping the Pain of Verbal Abuse – an 8 Step Program.* New York: John Wiley & Co. 1995.

Evans, Patricia. *Controlling People: How to Recognize, Understand, and Deal with People Who Try to Control You.* New York: Adams Media, 2002.

_____. *The Verbally Abusive Relationship.* Adams Media, 2010, 1996, 1992.

Herman, Judith, Ph.D. *Trauma and Recovery: The Aftermath of Violence from Domestic Abuse to Political Terror.* New York: Basic Books. 1992, 1997.

Hirigoyen, Marie- France. *Stalking the Soul: Emotional Abuse and the Erosion of Identity.* New York: Helen Marx Books, 2004.

Ketterman, Grace. *Verbal Abuse: Healing the Hidden Wound.* Ventura: Vine Books, 1993.

Kroeger, Catherine Clark. *No Place for Abuse: Biblical Practical Resources to Counteract Domestic Violence.* Wheaton: IVP Books, 2010.

_____ and Beck, J. R.(Eds.) *Women, Abuse and the Bible.* Ada: Baker Books, 1996.

Lerner, Harriet. *The Dance of Deception.* New York: Harper Collins, 1993.

Porterfield, Kay Marie. *Violent Voices:12 Steps to Freedom from Verbal and Emotional Abuse.* Deerfield Beach: Health Communications, 1989.

Raja, Sheela. *Trauma and PTSD Workbook.* Oakland: New Harbinger Press, 2012.

Roberts, Barbara. *Not Under Bondage: Biblical Divorce for Abuse, Adultery and Desertion.* Australia: Maschil Press, 2008.

Schaefer, Brenda. *Is It Love or Addiction*? Center City: Hazeldon, 1997.

Spangler, Tina Bakalar. *The Pulpit Bully.* iUniverse. 2015,

Tobias, Madeleine and Lalich, J. *Captive Hearts, Captive Minds: Freedom and recovery from cults and abusive relationships.* Alameda: Hunter House. 1994.

Other Resources

Arabi, Shadidi. Her writing about narcissism's effects and recovery is at thoughtcatalog.com and also at The Smart Girl's Guide to Self-Care found at @selfcarehaven.. 2018

Baird, Julia and Hayley Gleeson. *Shattering the Silence: Austrialians tell their stories of surviving domestic violence in the church.* mobile.abc.net.au. August 18, 2017.

Barnes, Zahira. *What's it's like to live with PTSD after escaping domestic violence.* www.self.com. April 19, 2018

Bassett, Scott. *Beating the narcissist.* SC Publishing. 2017. 3 videos at understandingnarcissism.com

Fortune, Marie. FaithTrust Institute. www.faithtrustinstitute.org

Haddad, Dr. Mimi. President, Christians for Biblical Equality. Publishes *Priscilla Papers*, a scholarly journal; Arise blog, fosters chapters, conferences, and other work on mutuality in the faith. cbeinternatonal.org.

Hennessey, Donald. *Awakening the Evangelical Church to domestic violence and abuse in its midst.* cryingoutforjustice.com

Holly, Kelly Jo. *Verbal Abuse Journals: Domestic violence and abuse exposed.* verbalabusejournals.com

Klein, Elizabeth. *'God Hates Divorce' is only part of the story.* crosswalk.com. July 14, 2017

McClaskey, Cyinthia. *Religion's Cell: Doctrines of the Church that lead to bondage and abuse.* 2013+ www.religionscell.com

Moss, Danni. *BECAUSE IT MATTERS-Freedom from abuse in Christianity.* June 20, 2010. dannimoss.wordpress.com

Nelson, Gwyneth. *My Abusive 'Christian' Marriage.* Today's Christian Woman. January, 2009.

Nunneley, Kate Wallace. *Five myths of male headship.* The Junia Project. December 16, 2015.

Rainer, Thom S. *Fourteen symptoms of toxic church leaders.* thomrainer.com. October 1, 2014.

Tchividjian, Boz. *Godly response to abuse in a Christian environment.* www.netgrace.org

VanVonderen, Jeff. *Spiritual Abuse Recovery Resources.* Christian Recovery International. 2018.spiritualabuserecovery.com. or http://jeffvanvonderen.com

Williams-Fields, Jennifer. *You can get PTSD from staying in an abusive relationship.* PTSD Journal, 2018.

CPSIA information can be obtained
at www.ICGtesting.com
Printed in the USA
LVHW101413021218
598971LV00006B/1060/P

9 781722 423131